Leaves
from My Journal

From the
Faith Promoting Series

By President Wilford Woodruff

Designed for the Instruction and
Encouragement of Young Latter-day Saints

←——————→

JUVENILE INSTRUCTOR OFFICE
Salt Lake City,
1881

ISBN 1-930679-37-8

Archive Publishers
Grantsville, Utah

PREFACE.

ON issuing "A STRING OF PEARLS," the second volume of the FAITH PROMOTING SERIES, some months since, it was announced that the next volume would be composed of sketches by President Wilford Woodruff. Since that time much impatience has been manifested by the Saints generally to have the volume published.

We now have much pleasure in offering it for public consideration, and trust that the young people who peruse it will be inspired to emulate in their lives the faith, perseverance and integrity that so distinguish its author.

Brother Woodruff is a remarkable man. Few men now living, who have followed the quiet and peaceful pursuits of life, have had such an interesting and eventful experience as he has. Few, if any in this age, have spent a more active and useful life. Certainly no man living has been more particular about recording with his own hand, in a daily journal, during half a century, the events of his own career and the things that have come under his observation. His elaborate journal has always been one of the principal sources from which the Church history has been compiled.

Possessed of wonderful energy and determination, and mighty faith, Brother Woodruff has labored long and with great success in the Church. He has ever had a definite object in view—to know the will of the Almighty and to do it. No amount of self-denial has been too great for him. Satan, knowing the power for good that Brother Woodruff would be, if permitted to live, has often sought to effect his destruction.

The adventures, accidents and hair-breadth escapes that he has met with, are scarcely equaled by the record that the former apostle, Paul, has left us of his life.

The power of God has been manifested in a most remarkable manner in preserving Brother Woodruff's life. Considering the number of bones he has had broken, and other bodily injuries he has received, it is certainly wonderful that now, at the age of seventy-four years, he is such a sound, well-preserved man. God grant that his health and usefulness may continue for many years to come.

Of course, this volume contains but a small portion of the interesting experience of Brother Woodruff's life, but very many profitable lessons may be learned from it, and we trust at some future time to be favored with other sketches from his pen.

What the next volume of the FAITH-PROMOTING SERIES will be, we are not prepared to say, but we promise that it will be issued soon, and that it will be both interesting and instructive.

THE PUBLISHER.

CONTENTS

CHAPTER 1.

CHAPTER II.

CHAPTER III.

CHAPTER IV.

CHAPTER V.

CHAPTER VI.

CHAPTER VII.

CHAPTER VIII.

CHAPTER IX.

CHAPTER X.

CHAPTER XI.

CHAPTER XII.

CHAPTER XXIII.

CHAPTER XXIV.

CHAPTER XXV.

CHAPTER I.

STRICTNESS OF THE "BLUE LAWS" OF CONNECTICUT--THE OLD PROPHET MASON — HIS VISION—HIS PROPHECY—HEAR THE GOSPEL, AND EMBRACE IT—VISIT KIRTLAND AND SEE JOSEPH SMITH—A WORK FOR THE OLD PROPHET.

FOR the benefit of the young Latter-day Saints, for whom the Faith-Promoting Series is especially designed, I will relate some incidents from my experience. I will commence by giving a short account of some events of my childhood and youth.

I spent the first years of my life under the influence of what history has called the "Blue Laws" of Connecticut. No man, boy, or child of any age was permitted to play, or do any work from sunset Saturday night until the sun had set on Sunday. After sunset had come Sunday evening men might work, and boys might jump, shout, and play as much as they pleased.

Our parents were very strict with us on Saturday night, and all day Sunday we had to sit very still and say over the Presbyterian catechism and some passages in the Bible.

The people of Connecticut in those days thought it wicked to believe in any religion, or belong to any church, except the Presbyterian. They did not believe in having any prophet, apostles, or revelations, as they had in the days of Jesus, and as we now have in the Church of Jesus Christ of Latter-day Saints.

There was one aged man in Connecticut, however, by the name of Robert Mason, who did not believe like the rest of the people. He believed it was necessary to have prophets, apostles, dreams, visions and revelations in the church of Christ, the same as they had who lived in ancient days; and he believed the Lord would raise up a people and a church, in the last days, with prophets, apostles and all the gifts, powers and blessings; which it ever contained in any age of the world.

The people called this man, the old prophet Mason. He frequently came to my father's house when I was a boy, and taught me and my brothers those principles; and I believed him.

This prophet prayed a great deal, and he had dreams and visions and the Lord showed him many things, by visions, which were to come to pass in the last days.

I will here relate one vision, which he related to me. The last time I ever saw him, he said: "I was laboring in my field at mid-day when I was enwrapped in a vision. I was placed in the midst of a vast forest of fruit trees: I was very hungry, and walked a long way through the orchard searching for fruit to eat, but I could not find any in the whole orchard and I wept because I could find no fruit. While I stood gazing at the orchard, and wondering why there was no fruit, the trees began to fall to the ground upon every side of me until there was not one tree standing in the whole orchard; and while I was marveling at the scene, I saw young sprouts start up from the roots of the trees which had fallen and they opened into young thrifty trees before my ayes. They budded, blossomed and bore fruit until the trees were loaded with the finest fruit I ever beheld and I rejoiced to see so much fine fruit. I stepped up to a tree and picked my hands full of fruit and marveled at its beauty, and as I was about to taste of it the vision closed and I found myself in the field in the same place I was at the commencement of the vision.

"I then knelt upon the ground and prayed unto the Lord and asked Him in the name of Jesus Christ to show me the meaning of the vision. The Lord said unto me: 'This is the interpretation of the vision: the great trees of the forest represent the generation of men in which you live. There is no church of Christ or kingdom of God upon the earth in your generation. There is no fruit of the church of Christ upon the earth. There is no man ordained of God to administer in any of the ordinances of the gospel of salvation upon the earth in this day and generation. But in the next generation, I the Lord will set up my kingdom and my church upon the earth and the fruits of the kingdom and church of Christ, such as have followed the prophets, apostles and saints in every dispensation shall again be found in all their fullness upon the earth. You will live to see the day and handle the fruit; but will never partake of it in the flesh.'"

When the old prophet had finished relating the vision and interpretation he said to me, calling me by my Christian name: "I shall never partake of this fruit in the flesh; but you will, and you will become a conspicuous actor in that kingdom." He then turned and left me. These were the last words he ever spoke to me upon the earth.

This was a very striking circumstance as I had spent many hours and days during twenty years with this old Father Mason, and he had never named this vision to me before, but at the beginning of this last conversation, he told me that he felt impelled by the Spirit of the Lord to relate it to me.

He had this vision about the year 1800, and he related it to me in 1830—the same spring that this Church was organized.

This vision, with his other teachings to me, made a great impression upon my mind, and I prayed a great deal to the Lord to lead me by His Spirit and prepare me for His church when it did come.

In 1832, I left Connecticut. and traveled with my eldest brother to Oswego County, New York; and in the winter of 1833, I saw for the first time in my life an Elder of the Church of Jesus Christ of Latter-day Saints. He preached in a school-house near where I lived. I attended the meeting, and the Spirit of the Lord bore record to me that what I heard was true. I invited the Elder to my house, and next day I, with my eldest brother, went down into the water and was baptized. We were the first two baptized in Oswego County, New York.

When I was baptized I thought of what the old prophet had said to me.

In the spring of 1834, I went to Kirtland, saw the Prophet Joseph Smith and went with him and with more than two hundred others in Zion's Camp, up to Missouri. When I arrived at my journey's end, I took the first opportunity and wrote a long letter to Father Mason and told him I had found the church of Christ that he had told me about. I told him about its organization and the coming forth of the Book of Mormon; that the Church had prophets, apostles, and all the gifts and blessings in it, and that the true fruit of the kingdom and church of Christ were manifest among the Saints as the Lord had shown him in his vision. He received my letter and read it over many times and handled it as he had handled the fruit in the vision; but he was very aged and soon died. He did not live to see any Elder to administer the ordinances of the gospel unto him.

The first opportunity I had, after the doctrine of baptism for the dead was revealed, I went forth and was baptized for him. He was a good man and a true prophet, for his prophecies have been fulfilled.

CHAPTER II.

PREPARING TO GO UP TO ZION—FIRST MEETING WITH PRESIDENT YOUNG—CAMP OF ZION STARTS—NUMBERS MAGNIFIED IN THE EYES OF BEHOLDERS—REMARKABLE DELIVERANCE — SELFISHNESS, AND ITS RE-WARD.

I ARRIVED at Kirtland on the 25th of April, 1834, and for the first time saw the Prophet Joseph

Smith. He invited me to his house. I spent about a week with him and became acquainted with him and his family, also with many of the Elders and Saints living in Kirtland, quite a number of whom were preparing to go up to Zion.

On Sunday, the 27th of April, I attended a meeting in a school-house in Kirtland and for the first time heard Elders Sidney Rigdon, Orson Hyde, Orson Pratt and others speak and bear testimony to the work of God, and much of the Spirit of God was poured out upon the Saints.

It was on the 26th of April, 1834, that I was first introduced to Elders Brigham Young and H. C. Kimball. When I met Brother Brigham he had his hands full of butcher knives; he gave me one and told me to go and put a good handle on it which I did. I also had a good sword, which Brother Joseph wanted, and I gave it to him. He carried it all the way in Zion's camp to Missouri and when he returned home he gave it back to me.

When I was called to go on a mission to the South I left the sword and knife with Lyman Wight. When he was taken prisoner at Far West with Joseph and Hyrum, he had both the sword and knife with him. All their weapons were taken from them, so were the arms of many of the Saints at Far West under promise that they should be returned to them when they were prepared to leave the state.

When the brethren went to get their arms, Father James Allred saw my sword which Lyman Wight had laid down and took it and left his own and afterwards gave it to me, and I still have it. I prize it because the Prophet Joseph carried it in Zion's Camp. The knife I never obtained.

The first day of May, 1834, was appointed for the Camp of Zion to start from Kirtland to go up to Missouri for the redemption of their brethren. Only a small portion of the Camp was ready. The Prophet told those who were ready to go to New Portage and wait for the remainder. I left in company with about twenty men with the baggage wagons. At night we pitched our tents. I went to the top of a hill and looked down upon the camp of Israel. I knelt upon the ground and prayed. I rejoiced and praised the Lord that I had lived to see some of the tents of Israel pitched, and a company gathered by the commandment of God to go up and help redeem Zion.

We tarried at New Portage until the 6th, when we were joined by the prophet and eighty-five more men. The day before they arrived, while passing through the village of Middlebury, the people tried to count them; but the Lord multiplied them in the eyes of the people so that those who numbered them said there were four hundred of them.

On the 7th Brother Joseph organized the camp

which consisted of about one hundred and thirty men. On the following day we continued our journey. We pitched our tent at night and had prayers night and morning. The Prophet told us every day what we should do.

We were nearly all young men, gathered from all parts of the country, and strangers to each other; but we got acquainted very soon, and had a happy time together.

It was a great school to us to be led by a Prophet of God a thousand miles through cities, towns, villages, and through the wilderness.

When persons stood by to count us they could not tell how many we numbered; some said five hundred, others one thousand.

Many were astonished as we passed through their towns. One lady ran to her door, pushed her spectacles to the top of her head, raised her hands, and exclaimed: "What under heavens has broken loose?" She stood in that position the last I saw of her.

The published history of Zion's Camp gives an account of the bones of a man which we dug out of a mound. His name was Zelph. The Lord showed the Prophet the history of the man in a vision. The arrow, by which he was killed, was found among his bones. One of his thigh bones was broken by a stone slung in battle. That bone was put into my wagon, and I carried it to Clay county, Missouri, and buried it in the earth.

The Lord delivered Israel in the days of Moses by dividing the Red Sea, so they went over dry shod. When their enemies tried to do the same, the water closed upon them and they were drowned. The Lord delivered Zion's Camp from their enemies on the 19th of June, 1834, by piling up the waters in Fishing River forty feet in one night so that our enemies could not cross. He also sent a great hail-storm which broke them up and sent them seeking for shelter.

The camp of Zion arrived at Brother Burk's, in Clay County, Missouri, on the 24th of June, 1834, and we pitched our tents on the premises. He told some of the brethren of my company that he had a spare room that some of us might occupy if we would clean it. Our company accepted the offer, and fearing some other company would get it first, left all other business and went to work, cleaned out the room, and immediately spread down our blankets, so as to hold a right to the room. It was but a short time afterwards that our brethren who were attacked by cholera were brought in and laid upon our beds. None of us ever used those blankets again, for they were buried with the dead. So we gained nothing but experience by being selfish, and we lost our bedding.

I will exhort all my young friends to not cherish selfishness; but if you have it, get rid of it as soon as possible. Be generous and noblehearted, kind to your parents, brothers, sisters and play-mates. Never contend with them; but try to make peace whenever you can. Whenever you are blessed with any good thing, be willing to share it with others. By cultivating these principles while you are young, you will lay a foundation to do much good through your lives and you will be beloved and respected of the Lord and all good men.

CHAPTER III.

ADVISED TO REMAIN IN MISSOURI—A DESIRE TO PREACH—PRAY TO THE LORD FOR A MISSION—PRAYER ANSWERED—SENT ON A MISSION TO ARKANSAS — DANGEROUS JOURNEY THROUGH JACKSON COUNTY— LIVING ON RAW CORN, AND SLEEPING ON THE GROUND — MY FIRST SERMON — REFUSED FOOD AND SHELTER BY A PRES-BYTERIAN PREACHER — WANDER THROUGH SWAMPS—ENTERTAINED BY INDIANS.

AFTER Joseph, the Prophet, had led Zion's Camp to Missouri, and we had passed through all the trials of that journey, and had buried a number of our brethren as recorded in history, the Prophet called the Camp together and organized the Church in Zion and gave much good counsel to all.

He advised all the young men who had not families to stay in Missouri and not return to Kirtland. Not having any family, I stopped with Lyman Wight, as did Milton Holmes and Heman Hyde. We spent the summer together, laboring hard, cutting wheat, quarrying rock, making brick, or anything else we could find to do. In the fall I had a desire to go and preach the gospel. I knew the gospel which the Lord had revealed to Joseph Smith was true and of such great value that I wanted to tell it to the people who had not heard it. It was so good and plain that it seemed to me I could make the people believe it.

I was but a Teacher, and it is not a Teacher's office to go abroad and preach. I dared not tell any of the authorities of the Church that I wanted to preach lest they might think I was seeking for an office.

I went into the woods where no one could see me and I prayed to the Lord to open my way so that I could go and preach the gospel. While I was praying, the Spirit of the Lord came upon me and told me my prayer was heard and that my request should be granted.

I felt very happy and got up and walked out of the woods into the traveled road and there I met a High Priest who had lived in the same house with me some six months.

He had not said a word to me about preaching the gospel; but now, as soon as I met him, he said, "the Lord has revealed to me that it is your privilege to be ordained and to go and preach the gospel."

I told him I was willing to do whatever the Lord required of me. I did not tell him I had just asked the Lord to let me go and preach.

In a few days a council was called at Lyman Wight's, and I was ordained a Priest and sent on a mission into Arkansas and Tennessee in company with an Elder. This mission was given us by Elder Edward Partridge who was the first Bishop ordained in the Church.

The law of God to us in those days was to go without purse or scrip. Our journey lay through Jackson County from which the Saints had just been driven, and it was dangerous for a "Mormon" to be found in that part of the State.

We put some Books of Mormon and some clothing into our valises, strapped them on our backs, and started on foot. We crossed the ferry into Jackson County and went through it.

In some instances the Lord preserved us as it were by miracle from the mob.

We dared not go to houses and get food so we picked and ate raw corn and slept on the ground, and did any way we could until we got out of the County.

We dared not preach while in that County and we did but little preaching in the State of Missouri. The first time I attempted to preach was on Sunday, in a tavern, in the early part of December, 1834. It was snowing at the time, and the room was full of people. As I commenced to speak the landlord opened the door, and the snow blew on the people; and when I inquired the object of having the door open in a snowstorm, he informed me that he wanted some light on the subject. I found it was the custom of the country.

How much good I did in that sermon I never knew, and probably never shall know until I meet that congregation in judgment.

In the southern portion of Missouri and the northern part of Arkansas, in 1834, there were but very few inhabitants.

We visited a place called Harmony Mission on the Osage River, one of the most crooked rivers in the west. This mission was kept by a Presbyterian minister and his family.

We arrived there on Sunday night at sunset. We had walked all day with nothing to eat and were very hungry and tired. Neither the minister nor his wife would give us anything to eat nor let us stay over night because we were "Mormons," and the only chance we had was to go twelve miles farther down the river, to an Osage Indian trading post kept by a Frenchman named Jereu. And this wicked priest, who would not give us a piece of bread, lied to us about the road and sent us across the swamp, and we wallowed knee-deep in mud and water till ten o'clock at night in trying to follow this crooked river. We then left the swamp and put out into the prairie to lie in the grass for the night.

When we came out of the swamp, we heard an Indian drumming on a tin pail and singing. It was very dark but we traveled towards the noise and when we drew near the Indian camp, quite a number of large Indian dogs came out to meet us. They smelt us, but did not bark nor bite.

We were soon surrounded by Osage Indians, and kindly received by Mr. Jereu and his wife who was an Indian. She gave us an excellent supper and a good bed which we were thankful for after the fatigue of the day.

As I laid my head on my pillow I felt to thank God from the bottom of my heart for the exchange of the barbarous treatment of a civilized Presbyterian priest, for the humane, kind and generous treatment of the savage Osage Indians.

May God reward them both according to their deserts.

CHAPTER IV.

A JOURNEY OF SIXTY MILES WITHOUT FOOD—CONFRONTED BY A BEAR—PASS UNHARMED—SURROUNDED BY WOLVES — LOST IN THE DARKNESS—REACH A CABIN— ITS INMATES—NO SUPPER—SLEEP ON THE FLOOR—THE HARDEST DAY'S WORK OF MY LIFE — TWELVE MILES MORE WITHOUT BREAKFAST — BREAKFAST AND ABUSE TOGETHER.

WE arose in the morning after a good night's rest. I was somewhat lame from wading in the swamp the night before. We had a good breakfast. Mr. Jereu sent an Indian to see us across the river and informed us that it was sixty miles to the nearest settlement of either white or red men.

We were too bashful to ask for anything to take with us to eat; so we crossed the river and started on our day's journey of sixty miles without a morsel of food of any kind. What for? To preach the gospel of Jesus Christ, to save this generation.

Think of this children; think of what the Presidency, the Apostles, and the Elders of this

Church have passed through to give you the homes and comforts you now enjoy.

Think of this, ye statesmen and judges of this American nation; ye who are now seeking to destroy God's people in the wilderness, who have gone hungry and naked and have labored for fifty years to save this nation and generation. Cease your exertions to destroy this people, or God will bring you to judgment and destroy your nation and cast you into outer darkness where there shall be weeping and gnashing of teeth; for the Lord God has spoken it. I must pause, I almost forgot I was writing a narrative.

We started about sunrise and crossed a thirty-mile prairie, apparently as level as a house floor without a shrub or water. We arrived at timber about two o'clock in the afternoon. As we approached the timber, a large black bear came out towards us. We were not afraid of him for we were on the Lord's business and had not mocked God's prophet as did the forty-two wicked children who said to Elisha "Go up thou bald head," for which they were torn by bears.

When the bear got within eight rods of us he sat on his haunches and looked at us a moment, and then ran away; and we went on our way rejoicing. We had to travel in the night which was cloudy and very dark, as we had great difficulty to keep the road. Soon a large drove of wolves gathered around us and followed us and came very close. At times it seemed as though they would eat us up.

We had materials for striking a fire and at ten o'clock, not knowing where we were, and the wolves becoming so bold, we thought it wisdom to make one; so we stopped and made a large fire of oak limbs that lay on the ground, and as our fire began to burn the wolves left us.

As we were about to lie down on the ground—for we had no blankets—we heard a dog bark.

My companion said it was a wolf; I said it was a dog: but soon we heard a cow bell. Then we took each a firebrand and went about a quarter of a mile and found the house which was sixty miles from where we started that morning.

It was an old log cabin, about twelve feet square, with no door but an old blanket was hung up in the door-way. There was no furniture except one bedstead upon which lay a woman, several children and several small dogs. A man lay on the bare floor with his feet to the fire place, and all were asleep. I went in and spoke to the man but it did not wake him. I stepped to him and laid my hand on his shoulder. The moment he felt the weight of my hand he jumped to his feet and ran around the room as though he was frightened; but he was quieted when we informed him we were friends.

The cause of this fright was that he had shot a panther a few nights before and he thought its mate had jumped upon him.

He asked us what we wanted; we told him we wished to stop with him all night and that would like something to eat. He informed us we might lie on the floor as he did, but that he had not a mouthful for us to eat as he had to depend on his gun to get breakfast for his family in the morning. So we lay on the bare floor and slept through a long, rainy night which was pretty hard after walking sixty miles without anything to eat. That was the hardest day's work of my life.

The man's name was Williams. He was in the mob in Jackson County; and after the Saints were driven out he with many others, went south.

We got up in the morning and walked in the rain twelve miles to the house of a man named Bemon who was also one of the mob from Jackson County. They were about sitting down to breakfast as we came in.

In those days it was the custom of the Missourians to ask you to eat, even if they intended to cut your throat as soon as you got through; so he asked us to take breakfast and we were very glad of the invitation.

He knew we were "Mormons;" and as soon as we began to eat he began to swear about the "Mormons." He had a large platter of bacon and eggs and plenty of bread on the table, and his swearing did not hinder our eating, for the harder he swore the harder we ate until we got our stomachs full; then we arose from the table, took our hats, thanked him for our breakfast, and the last we heard of him he was still swearing.

I trust the Lord will reward him for our breakfast.

CHAPTER V.

OUR ANXIETY TO MEET A SAINT—JOURNEY TO AKEMAN'S—DREAM—FIND MR. AKEMAN A RANK APOSTATE—HE RAISES A MOB— THREATENED WITH TAR, FEATHERS, ETC.—I WARN MR. AKEMAN TO REPENT—HE FALLS DEAD AT MY FEET—I PREACH HIS FUNERAL SERMON.

IN the early days of the Church, it was a great treat to an Elder in his travels through the country to find a "Mormon;" it was so with us. We were hardly in Arkansas when we heard of a family named Akeman. They were in Jackson County in the persecution. Some of the sons had been tied up there and whipped on the bare back with hickory switches by the mob. We heard of their living on Petit Jean River in the Arkansas Territory, and we went a long way to visit them.

There had recently been heavy rains and a creek that we had to cross was swollen to a rapid stream of eight rods in width. There was no person living nearer than two miles from the crossing and no boat. The people living at the last house on the road, some three miles from the crossing, said we would have to tarry till the water fell before we could cross. We did not stop, feeling to trust in God. Just as we arrived at the rolling flood, a negro on a powerful horse entered the stream on the opposite side and rode through it. On our making our wants known to him, he took us one at a time behind him and carried us safely over and we went on our way rejoicing.

We arrived that night within five miles of Mr. Akeman's and were kindly entertained by a stranger. During the night I had the following dream:

I thought an angel came to us, and told us we were commanded of the Lord to follow a certain straight path, which was pointed out to us—let it lead us wherever it might. After we had walked in it awhile we came to the door of a house which was in the line of a high wall running north and south so that we could not go around. I opened the door and saw the room was filled with large serpents; and I shuddered at the sight.

My companion said he would not go into the room for fear of the serpents. I told him I should try to go through the room though they killed me, for the Lord had commanded it. As I stepped into the room, the serpents coiled themselves up and raised their heads some two feet from the floor to spring at me. There was one much larger than the rest in the centre of the room which raised his head nearly as high as mine and made a spring at me. At that instant I felt as though nothing but the power of God could save me and I stood still. Just before the serpent reached me he dropped dead at my feet; all the rest dropped dead, swelled up, turned black, burst open, took fire and were consumed before my eyes, and we went through the room unharmed and thanked God for our deliverance.

I awoke in the morning and pondered upon the dream. We took breakfast, and started on our journey on Sunday morning to visit Mr. Akeman. I related to my companion my dream, and told him we should see something strange. We had great anticipations of meeting Mr. Akeman, supposing him to be a member of the Church. When we arrived at his house he received us very coldly, and we soon found that he had apostatized. He brought railing accusations against the Book of Mormon and the authorities of the Church.

Word was sent through all the settlements on the river for twenty miles that two "Mormon" preachers were in the place. A mob was soon raised and warning sent to us to leave immediately or we would be tarred and feathered, ridden on a rail and hanged. I soon saw where the serpents were. My companion wanted to leave; I told him no, I would stay and see my dream fulfilled.

There was an old gentleman and lady named Hubbel who had read the Book of Mormon and believed. Father Hubbel came to see us, and invited us to make our home with him while we stayed in the place. We did so and labored for him some three weeks with our axes clearing land, while we were waiting to see the salvation of God.

I was commanded of the Lord by the Holy Ghost to go and warn Mr. Akeman to repent of his wickedness. I did so, and each time he raged against me, and the last time he ordered me out of his house. When I went out he followed me and was very angry. When he came up to me, about eight rods from the house, he fell dead at my feet, turned black and swelled up just as I saw the serpent do in my dream.

His family, as well as ourselves, felt it was the judgment of God upon him. I preached his funeral sermon. Many of the mob died suddenly. We stayed about two weeks after Akeman's death and preached, baptized Mr. Hubbel and his wife, and then continued on our journey.

CHAPTER VI.

MAKE A CANOE—VOYAGE DOWN THE ARKANSAS RIVER—SLEEP IN A DE-SERTED TAVERN—ONE HUNDRED AND SEVENTY MILES THROUGH SWAMPS—FORTY MILES A DAY IN MUD KNEE-DEEP—A SUDDEN LAMENESS—LEFT ALONE IN AN ALLIGATOR SWAMP—HEALED IN ANSWER TO PRAYER— ARRIVAL AT MEMPHIS—AN ODD-LOOKING PREACHER—COMPELLED TO PREACH— POWERFUL AID FROM THE SPIRIT—NOT WHAT THE AUDIENCE EXPECTED.

WE concluded to go down Arkansas river and cross into Tennessee. We could not get passage on the boat because of low water, so we went on the bank of the river and cut down a sound cottonwood tree three feet through, and cut off a twelve-foot length from the butt end; and in two days we dug out a canoe. We made a pair of oars and a rudder, and on the 11th of March, 1835, we launched our canoe and commenced our voyage down the Arkansas river without provisions.

The first day we sailed twenty-five miles and stopped at night with a poor family who lived on the bank of the river. These kind folks gave us supper and breakfast, and in the morning gave us a johnny-cake and piece of pork to take with us on our journey.

We traveled about fifty miles that day and at night stopped at an old deserted tavern in a village called Cadron, which was deserted because it was believed to be haunted by evil spirits.

We made a fire in the tavern, roasted a piece of our pork, ate our supper, said our prayers, went into a chamber, lay down on the bare floor, and were soon asleep.

I dreamed I was at my father's house in a good feather bed and I had a good night's rest. When I awoke, the bed vanished, and I found myself on the bare floor and well rested, not having been troubled with evil spirits or anything else.

We thanked the Lord for His goodness to us, ate the remainder of our provisions and continued our journey down the river to Little Rock, the capital of Arkansas, which then con-sisted of only a few cabins.

After visiting the place, we crossed the river and tied up our canoe which had carried us safely one hundred and fifty miles.

We then took the old military road leading from Little Rock to Memphis, Tennessee. This road lay through swamps, and was covered with mud and water most of the way for one hundred and seventy miles. We walked forty miles in a day through mud and water knee-deep.

On the 24th of March, after traveling some ten miles through mud, I was taken lame with a sharp pain in my knee. I sat down on a log. My companion, who was anxious to get to his home in Kirtland, left me sitting in an alligator swamp. I did not see him again for two years. I knelt down in the mud and prayed and the Lord healed me; and I went on my way rejoicing.

On the 27th of March, I arrived at Memphis, weary and hungry. I went to the best tavern in the place kept by Mr. Josiah Jackson. I told him I was a stranger and had no money. I asked him if he would keep me over night.

He asked me what my business was and I told him I was a preacher of the gospel. He laughed, and said that I did not look much like a preacher. I did not blame him, as all the preachers he had ever been acquainted with rode on fine horses or in fine carriages, clothed in broadcloth, and had large salaries, and would see this whole world sink to perdition before they would wade through one hundred and seventy miles of mud to save the people.

The landlord wanted a little fun, so he said he would keep me if I would preach. He wanted to see if I could preach.

I must confess that by this time I became a little mischievous, and plead with him not to set me preaching.

The more I plead to be excused, the more determined Mr. Jackson was that I should preach. He took my valise and the landlady got me a good supper.

I sat down in a large hall to eat supper. Before I got through, the room began to be filled by some of the rich and fashionable of Memphis, dressed in their broadcloth and silk, while my appearance was such as you can imagine after traveling through the mud as I had been.

When I had finished eating, the table was carried out of the room over the heads of the people. I was placed in the corner of the room with a stand having a Bible, hymn book and candle on it, hemmed in by a dozen men, with the landlord in the center.

There were present some five hundred persons who had come together, not to hear a gospel sermon but to have some fun.

Now, boys, how would you like this position? On your first mission, without a companion or friend, and to be called upon to preach!

preach to such a congregation! With me it was one of the most pleasing hours of my life, although I felt as though I should like company.

I read a hymn and asked them to sing. Not a soul would sing a word.

I told them I had not the gift of singing ; but with the help of the Lord, I would both pray and preach. I knelt down to pray, and the men around me dropped on their knees. I prayed to the Lord to give me His Spirit and to show me the hearts of the people. I promised the Lord in my prayer that I would deliver to that congregation whatever He would give. I arose and spoke one hour and a half, and it was one of the best sermons of my life.

The lives of the congregation were opened to the vision of my mind, and I told them of their wicked deeds and the reward they would obtain. The men who surrounded me dropped their heads. Three minutes after I closed, I was the only person in the room.

Soon I was shown to a bed in a room adjoining a large one in which were assembled many of the men whom I had been preaching to. I could hear their conversation.

One man said he would like to know how that "Mormon" boy knew of their past lives.

In a little while they got to disputing about some doctrinal point. One suggested calling me to decide the point. The landlord said, "no; we have had enough for once."

In the morning, I had a good breakfast. The landlord said if I came that way again to stop at his house and stay as long as I might choose.

CHAPTER VII.

CURIOUS WORSHIP—MEET ELDER PARRISH —LABOR TOGETHER IN TENNESSEE— ADVENTURE IN BLOODY RIVER—A NIGHT OF PERIL—PROVIDENTIAL LIGHT —MENACED BY A MOB--GOOD ADVICE FROM A BAPTIST PREACHER—SUMMARY OF LABORS FOR THE YEAR.

AFTER leaving Memphis, I traveled through the country to Benton County, and preached on the way as I had opportunity.

I stopped one night with a Squire Hardman, an Episcopalian. Most of the night was spent by the family in music and dancing. In the morning, at the breakfast table, Mr. Hardman asked me if we believed in music and dancing.

I told him we did not really consider them essential to salvation.

He said he did, and therefore should not join our Church.

On the 4th of April, 1835, I had the happy privilege of meeting Elder Warren Parrish at the house of Brother Frys. He had been preaching in that part of Tennessee, in company with David W. Patten, and had baptized a number and organized several small branches.

Brother Patten had returned home and Brother Parrish was laboring alone. I joined him in the ministry, and we labored together three months and nineteen days when he was called to Kirtland.

During the time we were together, we traveled through several Counties in Tennessee for the distance of seven hundred and sixty miles, and preached the gospel daily as we had opportunity. We baptized some twenty persons. By the counsel of the Prophet Joseph Smith and Oliver Cowdery, Elder Parrish ordained me an Elder and left me to take charge of the branches that had been raised up in that neighborhood.

As soon as I was left alone, I extended my circuit and labors. For a season I had large congregations; many seemed to believe and I baptized a number.

On the 15th of August, I had an appointment at the house of Brother Taylor, the step-father of Abraham 0. Smoot.

I had to cross Bloody River, which I had to swim in consequence of heavy rains. While crossing, my horse became entangled in a tree top and almost drowned; but I succeeded in getting him loose.

We swam to the shore separately. He reached the shore first and waited till I came out. I got into the saddle and went on my way in good spirits, and had a good meeting.

On the 20th of October, I baptized three Campbellites, one of whom was a deacon. I then rode twelve miles to Mr. Greenwood's who was eighty years old and had been a soldier under General Washington. His wife, who was ninety-three years old, I found quite smart and busy carding wool. I preached at their house and baptized both of them.

On the following day I preached at the house of Benjamin L. Clapp and baptized seven Campbellites and one Baptist. On the 16th of November, I preached at Brother Camps and baptized three. On the day following, it being Sunday, I preached again at Brother Clapp's and baptized five. At the close of the meeting I mounted my horse to ride to Clark's River in company with Seth Utley, four other brethren and two sisters. The distance was twenty miles.

We came to a stream which was so swollen by rains that we could not cross without swimming our horses. To swim would not be safe for the females, so we went up the stream to find a ford. In the attempt we were overtaken by a severe storm of wind and rain and lost our way in the darkness and wandered through creeks and mud. But the Lord does not forsake His Saints in any of their troubles. While we were in the woods suffering under the blast of the storm, groping like the blind for the wall, a bright light suddenly shone around us and revealed to us our dangerous situation on the edge of a gulf. The light continued with us until we found the road; we then went on our way rejoicing, though the darkness returned and the rain continued.

We reached Brother Henry Thomas' in safety about nine o'clock at night, having been five hours in the storm and forded streams many times. None of us felt to complain; but were thankful to God for His preserving care.

On the following day, I preached in Damon Creek and organized a branch called the Damon Creek Branch, and ordained Daniel Thomas a teacher.

On the 19th of December, I again preached at the house of Brother Clapp and baptized five persons; one was a Campbellite preacher.

On the following day, I preached at the house of Brother Henry Thomas, when a mob of about fifty persons collected, headed by a Baptist preacher, who, after asking one question, advised the mob to not lay hands on any man on account of his principles.

The advice was good and well taken.

At the close of the meeting, I baptized three persons, one seventy-eight years old.

This brings the year 1835 to a close—the first year of my mission—during which time I had traveled three thousand two hundred and forty-eight miles, held one hundred and seventy meetings, baptized forty-three persons—three of whom were Campbellite preachers—assisted Elder Parrish to baptize twenty more, confirmed thirty-five, organized three branches, ordained two Teachers and one Deacon, procured thirty subscribers for the Messenger and Advocate, one hundred and seventy-three signers to the petition to the governor of Missouri for redress of wrongs done the Saints in Jackson County, had three mobs rise against me—but was not harmed, wrote eighteen letters, received ten, and finally closed the labors of the year 1835, by eating johnny-eake, butter and honey at Brother A. O. Smoot's.

CHAPTER VIII.

STUDY GRAMMAR—MEET ELDER PATTEN —
GLORIOUS NEWS—LABOR WITH A. O.
SMOOT—TURNED OUT OF A MEETING HOUSE
BY A BAPTIST PREACHER—PREACH IN THE
OPEN AIR—GOOD RESULT—ADVENTURE ON
THE TENNESSEE RIVER—A NOVEL CHARGE
TO ARREST AND CONDEMN MEN UPON—MOB
POISONS OUR HORSES.

I SPENT the fore part of January, 1836, (the
weather being very cold) at the house of A. O.
Smoot, in Kentucky, studying Kirkham's English
Grammar. I continued to travel and preach in
Kentucky and Tennessee and baptized all that
would believe my testimony.

On the 26th of February, we held a
conference at the house of Brother Lewis Clapp
(father of B. L. Clapp). There were represented
one hundred and three members in that mission. I
ordained A. O. Smoot and Benjamin Boydston
Elders, and Daniel Thomas and Benjamin L. Clapp
Priests. I also ordained one Teacher and two
Deacons.

After conference, I took Brothers Smoot and
Clapp with me to preach. The former was with me

constantly till the 21st of April, when we had the privilege of meeting with Elder David W. Patten who had come direct from Kirtland, and who had been ordained one of the Twelve Apostles.

It was a happy meeting. He gave us an account of the endowment at Kirtland, the glorious blessings received, the ministration of angels, the organization of the Twelve Apostles and Seventies, and informed me that I was appointed a member of the second quorum of Seventies. All of this was glorious news to me and caused my heart to rejoice.

On the 28th of May, we were joined by Elder Warren Parrish, direct from Kirtland. We had a happy time together.

On the 28th, we held a conference at Brother Seth Utley's, where were represented all the branches of the Church in the South.

I was ordained on the 31st of May a member of the second quorum of Seventies under the hands of David W. Patten and • Warren Parrish.

At the close of the conference, we separated for a short time. Elders Patten and Parrish labored in Tennessee, Brother Smoot and myself in Kentucky. On the 9th of June, we all met at Damon Creek Branch where Brother Patten baptized two. One was Father Henry Thomas who had been a revolutionary soldier under General Washington, and father of Daniel and Henry

Thomas.

A warrant was issued, on the oath of a priest, against David W. Patten, W. Parrish and myself. We were accused in the warrant of the great "crime" of testifying that Christ would come in this generation, and that we promised the Holy Ghost to those whom we baptized. Brother Patten and Parrish were taken on the 19th of June, I being in another County, escaped being arrested. The brethren were put under two thousand dollars bonds to appear at court. Albert Petty and Seth Utley were their bondsmen.

They were tried on the 22nd of June. They plead their own cause. Although men came forward and testified they did receive the Holy Ghost after they were baptized, the brethren were condemned; but were finally released by paying the expenses of the mob court.

There was one peculiar circumstance connected with this trial by a mob court, which was armed to the teeth. When the trial was through with, the people were not willing to permit more than one to speak. Warren Parish had said but few words, and they were not willing to let David Patten speak. But he, feeling the injustice of the court, and being filled with the power of God, arose to his feet and delivered a speech of about twenty minutes, holding them spellbound while he told them of their wickedness and the abominations

that they were guilty of; also of the curse of God
that awaited them if they did not repent for taking
up two harmless, inoffensive men for preaching the
gospel of Christ.

When he had got through his speech, the
judge said, "You must be armed with secret
weapons, or you would not talk in this fearless
manner to an armed court."

Brother Patten replied: "I have weapons that
you know not of, and they are given me of God, for
He gives me all the power I have."

The judge seemed willing to get rid of them
almost upon any terms, and offered to dismiss
them if their friends would pay the costs, which the
brethren present freely offered to do.

When the two were released, they mounted
their horses and rode a mile to Seth Utley's; but, as
soon as they had left, the court became ashamed
that they had been let go so easily and the whole
mob mounted their horses to follow them to Utley's.

One of the brethren, seeing the state of
affairs, went on before the mob to notify the
brethren so that they had time to ride into the
woods near by.

They traveled along about three miles to
Brother Gilbert Petty's and went to bed. The night
was dark, and they fell asleep.

But Brother Patten was warned in a dream
to get up and flee, as the mobs would soon be

there. They both arose, saddled their animals, and rode into the adjoining County.

The house they had just left was soon surrounded by the mob, but the brethren had escaped through the mercy of God.

I was invited to hold a meeting at a Baptist meeting house on the 27th of June. On my arrival I met a large congregation; but, on commencing meeting, Parson Browning ordered the meeting to be closed. I told the people I had come ten miles to preach the gospel to them and was willing to stand in a cart, on a pile of wood, on a fence, or any other place they would appoint, to have that privilege.

One man said he owned the fence and land in front of the meeting-house, and we might use both, for he did not believe that "Mormonism" would hurt either.

So the congregation crossed the road, took down the fence and made seats of it, and I preached to them one hour and a half. At the close Mr. Randolph Alexander bore testimony to the truth of what had been said. He invited me home with him, bought a Book of Mormon, and was baptized, and I organized a branch in that place.

On the 18th of July, Brother A. O. Smoot and I arrived at a ferry on the Tennessee River, and as the ferryman was not at home, the woman kindly gave us permission to use the ferryboat.

We led our horses on board and took the oars to cross the river. Brother Smoot had never used an oar, and I had not for some years, so we made awkward work of it. Soon he broke one oar and I let another fall overboard which left us only one broken oar to get to shore with. We narrowly escaped running into a steamboat. We struck shore half a mile below the landing place, tied up the boat, jumped on the bank with our horses, and went on our way with blistered hands, thankful to get on so well.

On Sunday, the 31st of July, A. O. Smoot and I preached at Mr. David Crider's, Weakly County, Tennessee. After the meeting, Mr. Crider was baptized. A mob gathered and threatened us, and poisoned our horses so that the one I rode, belonging to Samuel West, died a few days after. This horse had carried me thousands of miles while preaching the gospel.

I continued to travel with Brothers Smoot, Patten and Parrish in Tennessee and Kentucky, and we baptized all who would receive our testimony.

On the 2nd day of September, we held a general conference at the Damon Creek Branch. Elder Thomas B. Marsh, President of the Twelve Apostles, presided. All the branches in Tennessee and Kentucky were represented.

Brothers Randolph Alexander, Benjamin L. Clapp and Johnson F. Lane were ordained Elders and Lindsay Bradey was ordained to the lesser priesthood.

I assisted President Marsh to obtain fifteen hundred dollars from the Southern brethren to enter land in Missouri for the Church. The brethren made me a present of fifty dollars which I sent by President Marsh to enter forty acres of land for me. Elder Smoot and I were released from the Southern mission with permission to go to Kirtland.

CHAPTER IX.

ATTEND SCHOOL—MARRIAGE—IMPRESSED TO TAKE A MISSION TO FOX ISLANDS— ADVISED TO GO—JOURNEY TO CANADA— CASES OF HEALING — JOURNEY TO CON- NECTICUT — MY BIRTHPLACE — MOTHER'S GRAVE—BAPTIZE RELATIVES—JOINED BY MY WIFE—JOURNEY ON FOOT TO MAINE — ARRIVAL AT FOX ISLAND.

HAVING returned from my Southern mission in the autumn of 1836, in company with Elders A. O. Smoot and Jesse Turpin, I spent the following winter in Kirtland.

During this time I received my endowments and attended the school of Professor Haws who sor Haws who taught Greek, Latin and English grammar. I confined my studies mostly to Latin and English grammar.

This winter and the following spring, in some respects, may be regarded as one of the most interesting periods of the history of the Church, when we consider the endowments and teachings given in the temple, and the great apostasy which followed.

I was married to Miss Phoebe Whitmore Carter on the 13th of April, 183l, and received my patriarchal blessing under the hands of Father Joseph Smith, the Patriarch, two days later.

I felt impressed by the Spirit of God to take a mission to the Fox Islands situated east of the Maine shore, a country I knew nothing about. I made my feelings known to the Apostles and they advised me to go.

Feeling that it was my duty to go upon this mission, I did not tarry at home one year after having married a wife as the law of Moses would have allowed. On the contrary, I started just one month and one day after that important event, leaving my wife with Sister Hale, with whom she expected to stay for a season.

I left Kirtland in good spirits in company with Elder Jonathan H. Hale, and walked twelve miles to Fairport where we were joined by Elder Milton Holmes. There went aboard the steamer *Sandusky*, and made our way to Buffalo and pro-

ceeded thence to Syracuse by way of the Erie
Canal. We then walked to Richland, Oswego Co.,
N. Y., where I met my two brothers whom I had not
seen for several years.

After spending one night there, we
continued our journey to Sackett's Harbor, and
crossed Lake Ontario on the steamer *Oneida*, to
Kingston, Upper Canada, and from there also by
steamer along the canal to Jones' Falls, whence
we walked to a place called Bastard, Leeds
County.

Here we found a branch of the Church
presided over by John E. Page and James
Blakesly. We accompanied them to their place of
meeting, and attended a conference with them, at
which three hundred members of the Church were
represented.

Thirty-two persons presented themselves for
ordination whom I was requested to ordain in
company with Elder Wm. Draper. We ordained
seven Elders, nine Priests, eleven Teachers and
five Deacons.

We spoke to the people several times during
this conference, and at its close we were called
upon to administer to a woman who was
possessed of the devil. At times she was dumb
and greatly afflicted with the evil sprits that dwelt in
her. She believed in Jesus and in us as His
servants, and wished us to administer to her. Four
of us laid our hands on her head and commanded

the devil, in the name of Jesus Christ to depart out of her. It was immediately done and the woman arose with great joy and gave thanks and praise unto God; for, according to her faith, she was made whole from that hour.

A child also that was sick, was healed by the laying on of hands according to the word of God.

We walked thirty miles to visit another branch of the Saints at Leeds where we met with John Gordon and John Snider. Here we held a meeting and bore our testimony to the people.

A Sister Carns here came to us and requested to have the ordinance for the healing of the sick performed for two of her children who were afflicted. One was a suckling child which was lying at the point of death. I took it in my arms and presented it before the Elders who laid their hands upon it and it was made whole immediately; and I handed it back to the mother entirely healed.

We afterwards laid hands upon the other and it was also healed. It was done by the power of God, in the name of Jesus Christ, and the parents praised God for His goodness.

After leaving the Saints in this place, we returned to Kingston and crossed Lake Ontario in company with Isaac Russell, John Goodson and John Snider.

Brother Russell seemed to be constantly troubled with evil spirits which followed him when he subsequently went upon a mission to England, where Apostles Orson Hyde and Heber C. Kimball, when administering to him, had a severe contest with them, as Brother Kimball has related in his history.

Brothers Russell, Goodson and Snider continued with us to Schenectady where they left us to proceed to New York to join Elders Kimball and Hyde to go upon their mission to England.

After leaving these brethren, we traveled by rail to Albany and walked from there to Canaan, Conn., where we found a branch of the Church, including Jesse and Julian Moses and Francis K. Benedict. We held a two days' meeting with the Saints in Canaan, and I ordained Julian Moses and Francis K. Benedict Elders.

After holding several meetings in the town of Colebrook, and visiting my half siater, Eunice Woodruff, who was teaching school there, I proceeded to Avon, the place of my birth. There I visited many of my former neighbors and relatives, and the grave of my mother, Bulah Woodruff, who died June 11, 1808, when twenty-six years of age. The following verse was upon her tombstone:

"A pleasing form, a generous heart,
A good companion, just without art;
Just in her dealings, faithful to her friend,
Beloved in life, lamented in the end."

At the close of the day, I walked six miles to Farmington, where my father Aphek Woodruff was living, and I had the happy privilege of once more meeting with him and my step-mother, whom I had not seen for seven years. They greeted me with great kindness, and it was a happy meeting.

After visiting with my father a day or two, I returned to Avon where most of my relatives lived, and held meetings with them; and on the 12th of June, 1837, I baptized my uncle, Ozem Woodruff, his wife Hannah, and his son John, and we rejoiced together for this was in fulfillment of a dream that I had in 1818 when I was eleven years of age.

On the 15th of July, I had an appointment to preach at the house of my uncle, Adna Hart. While there, I had the happy privilege of meeting with my wife, Phoebe W. Woodruff, who had come from Kirtland to meet me and accompany me to her father's home in Scarboro, Maine.

Those who had assembled to hear me preach were relatives, neighbors and former friends. After meeting, we returned to Farmington to my father's home, where I spent the night with my father, step-mother, sister and wife. Elder Hale was also with us.

On the 19th of July, Elder Hale left us to go to his friends in New Rowley, Mass., and on the same evening I held a meeting in the Methodist meeting-house in the town of Farmington. I had a large congregation of citizens with whom I had been acquainted from my youth. My parents, wife and sister attended the meeting. The congregation seemed satisfied with the doctrines I taught, and they requested me to hold another meeting; but I felt anxious to continue my journey, and on the 20th of July, I parted with my father, step-mother and sister, and took stage for Hartford with my wife.

On my arrival at Hartford, not having money to pay the fare of both of us, I paid my wife's fare to Rowley, Mass., where there was a branch of the Church presided over by Brother Nathaniel Holmes, father of Jonathan and Milton Holmes, and I journeyed on foot.

The first day I walked fifty-two miles, the second day forty-eight, and the third day thirty-six miles, and arrived at Rowley at two o'clock, making 136 miles in a little over two-and-a-half days.

I spent eight days at New Rowley, holding meetings and visiting the Saints, including the Holmes family, and left there on the 1st of August.

On the 8th of August, in company with my wife and Elder Hale, I visited my wife's father, Ezra Carter, and his family in Scarboro, Maine, it being the first time I had ever seen any of her relatives. We were very kindly received.   My wife had been absent from her father's home about one year.

I spent eight days with Father Carter and household and one day I went out to sea with Fabian and Ezra Carter, my brothers-in-law, in a boat to fish with hooks. We caught 250 cod, haddock and hake, and we saw four whales, two at a time, it being the first time in my life I had ever seen the kind of a fish which is said to have swallowed Jonah.

On the 18th of August, 1837, I parted with my wife and her father's household, leaving her with them, and in company with Jonathan H. Hale, started upon the mission that I had in view when I left Kirtland.

We walked ten miles to Portland and took passage on the steamboat *Bangor* which carried us to Owl's Head where we went on board of a sloop which landed us on North Fox Island at 2 o'clock, a.m. on the 20th.

CHAPTER X.

DESCRIPTION OF VINAL HAVEN—POPULA-TION AND PURSUIT OF THE PEOPLE—GREAT VARIETY OF FISH—THE INTRODUCTION OF THE GOSPEL.

THE town of Vinal Haven includes both North and South Fox Islands, in lat. 44o north, and long. 69o 10' east. The population numbered, at the time of my visit, about l,800. The inhabi-tants were intelligent and industrious, and hospi-table to strangers. They get most of their wealth and living by fishing. The town fitted out over one hundred licensed sailing vessels, besides smaller craft.

North Fox Island is nine miles long by two miles in width, and had a population of 800. They had a post office, one store, a Baptist church and meeting-house, four school-houses and a tide grist mill.

The land was rather poor, yet there were some good farms. The products were wheat, barley, oats, potatoes and grass. The principal timber was fir, spruce, hemlock and birch. Raspberries and gooseberries grew in great abundance, and some up-land cranberries were raised. The principal stock of the island were sheep.

South Fox Island comes as near being without any definite form as any spot on earth I ever saw. It would be difficult for any person to describe it. It is about ten miles in length by five in width, and is one universal mass of rocks, formed into shelves, hills, and valleys, and cut up into necks and points to make room for the coves and harbors that run through and through the island.

The population was 1,000. The inhabitants got their living entirely by fishing. There is no chance for farming upon the island, and but a few garden patches which are cultivated at great expense. Some few sheep are raised there. Many of the inhabitants fish in the region of Newfoundland, and bring their fish home and cure them on flakes and prepare them for the market. They supply the market with great quantities of cod, mackerel and boxed herring.

Upon this island there were two stores, three tide saw mills, six school houses and a small branch of the Methodist church presided over by a priest. What timber there is upon this island such as pine, fir, spruce, hemlock and birch, and the whortleberries, raspberries and gooseberries, mostly grow out of the cracks of the rocks.

Great quantities of fish in almost endless varieties, inhabit the coves and harbors around the island. The whale, blackfish, shark, ground shark, pilot-fish, horse mackerel, sturgeon, salmon, halibut, cod, pollock, tom cod, hake, haddock, mackerel, shad, bass, alewife, herring, pohagen, dolphin, whiting, frost-fish, flounders, smelt, skate, shrimp, skid, cusk, blueback, scollop, dogfish, muttonfish, lumpfish, squid, five-fingers, monkfish, horsefish, sunfish, swordfish, thrasher, cat, scuppog, tootog, eyefish, cunner, ling, also the eel, lobster, clam, muscle, periwinkle, porpoise, seal, etc., are found there.

Thus I have given a brief description of Vinal Haven. It was quite dark when we landed there, without a farthing in money. We made our way over the rocks and through the cedars the best way we could until we found a house, when we rapped at the door. A woman put her head out of the window and asked who was there and what was wanted.

I told her we were two strangers, and wanted a bed to lie down upon until morning.

She let us in and gave us a bed, and we slept until quite late, it being Sunday morning. When we came out and took breakfast, it was nearly noon. I asked her what she charged for our entertainment, and she replied that we were welcome.

I then asked her if there was any religion or minister or church on the island. She informed me there was a Baptist minister by the name of Newton who had a congregation and meeting-house about five miles from there.

We thanked her for her kindness, walked to the meeting-house and stepped inside the doorway. We stood there until a deacon came to the door, when I asked him to go and tell the minister in the pulpit that there were two servants of God at the door who had a message to deliver to that people and wished the privilege of delivering it.

He sent for us to come to the pulpit, so we walked through the congregation with our valises under our arms and took a seat by the side of the minister who was about to speak as we came to the door.

He arose and delivered his discourse to the people, occupying about half an hour. When he closed he asked me what was my wish.

I told him we wished to speak to the people at any hour that would suit his or their convenience; so he gave notice that there were two strangers present who would speak to the people at five o'clock that evening.

We were quite a source of wonderment to the people as they had no idea who we were.

Mr. Newton asked us home to tea with him and we gladly accepted the invitation. When we arrived at his house, I opened my valise and took out the Bible, Book of Mormon and Doctrine and Covenants, laid them upon the table, and took my seat.

Mr. Newton took up the books and looked at them, but said nothing. I then asked him if there were any school-houses upon the island, and if so, whether they were free to preach in.

He answered that there were four, numbered respectively from one to four, and that they were free.

Mr. Newton and family accompanied us to the meeting-house where we met a large congregation, none of whom knew who we were or anything about our profession, except the minister.

Elder Hale and I went into the stand, and I arose with peculiar feelings and addressed the congregation for one hour, taking for my text Galatians 1:8-9.

This was the first time that I or any other Elder of the Church of Jesus Christ of Latter-day Saints had (to my knowledge) attempted to preach the fullness of the gospel and the Book of Mor-mon to the inhabitants of any island of the sea.

I had much liberty in speaking, and informed the people that the Lord had raised up a prophet and organized His Church as in the days of Christ and the ancient apostles, with prophets, apostles and the gifts as anciently, and that He had brought forth the Book of Mormon.

At the close of my remarks, Elder Hale bore testimony. I gave liberty for any one to speak that might wish to. As no one responded, I announced that we would hold meetings the next four evenings in the school-houses, beginning at No.1.

CHAPTER XI.

MR. NEWTON, THE BAPTIST PREACHED, WRESTLING WITH OUR TESTIMONY — REJECTS IT, AND BEGINS TO OPPOSE — SENDS TO A METHODIST MINISTER TO HELP HIM—MR. DOUGLASS' SPEECH—OUR GREAT SUCCESS ON THE NORTH ISLAND—GO TO THE SOUTH ISLAND AND BAPTIZE MR. DOUGLASS' FLOCK — GREAT NUMBERS OF ISLANDS — BOILED CLAMS — DAY OF PRAYER—CODFISH FLAKES.

DURING the first thirteen days of our sojourn upon the island, we preached seventeen discourses, being invited by the people to tarry with them. I left a copy of the Doctrine and Covenants with Mr. Newton for his perusal.

He read it, and the Spirit of God bore testimony to him of its truth. He pondered over it for days, and he walked his room until midnight trying to decide whether to receive or reject it.

He and his family attended about a dozen of my first meetings, and then he made up his mind, contrary to the dictation of the Spirit of God to him, to reject the testimony and come out against me. However, we commenced baptizing his flock.

The first two we baptized were a sea captain by the name of Justin Eames and his wife. Brother Jonathan H. Hale went down into the sea and baptized them on the 3rd of September, and these were the first baptisms performed by proper authority upon any of the islands of the sea (to my knowledge) in this dispensation.

Before we left Kirtland, some of the leading apostates there had tried to discourage Brother Hale about going upon his mission, telling him he would never baptize any one and he had better remain at home. When Captain Eames offered himself for baptism, I told Brother Hale to go and baptize him, and prove those men false prophets, and he did so.

On the following Sabbath, I baptized his brother, Ebenezer Eames, another sea captain, and a young lady. Mr. Newton, the Baptist minister, now commenced a war against us, and sent to the South Island for a Mr. Douglass, a Methodist minister (with whom he had been at variance for years) to come over and help him put down "Mormonism."

Mr. Douglass came over and they got as many people together as they could and held a conference. He railed against Joseph the prophet, and the Book of Mormon, and, taking that book in his hand with out-stretched arm, declared that he feared none of the judgments of God that would come upon him for rejecting it as the word of God.

(I never heard what his sentiments upon this subject were at the end of his term of fourteen years' imprisonment in the Thomaston Penitentiary, for an outrage upon his daughter, the judgment of which was given upon the testimony of his wife and daughter).

I was present and heard Mr. Douglass' speech upon this occasion and took minutes of the same. When he closed, I arose and informed the people that I would meet with them next Sunday in the meeting-house and answer Mr. Douglass, and wished him as well as the people to be present.

I informed the people that Mr. Douglass had made many false statements against Joseph Smith and the Latter-day Saints with whom he had no acquaintance, and he had misquoted much scripture, all of which I could correct.

We continued to baptize the people on the North Island until we had baptized every person who owned an interest in the Baptist meeting-house. I then followed Mr. Douglass home to the South Island and preached the gospel to and baptized nearly all the members of his church.

The excitement became great upon both islands, and on Sunday, the 17th of September, I met a large assembly from both islands and took the same subject that Mr. Douglass had dwelt upon in his remarks against the Book of Mormon and our principles.

I spoke two-and-a-half hours and answered every objection against the Book of Mormon, Joseph Smith or our principles.

I had good attention, and the people seemed satisfied. At the close of the meeting, Elder Hale administered the ordinance of baptism.

Mr. Newton, in order to save his cause, went to the main-land and brought over several ministers with him and held a protracted meeting. They hoped by this to stop the work of God—but all to no avail for the whole people would attend our meeting and receive the word of God and we continued to baptize.

We visited the dwellings of most of the inhabitants during our sojourn there.

Upon one occasion, while standing upon Mr. Carver's farm on the east end of the North Island, we counted fifty-five islands in that region, the majority of which were not inhabited. We also saw twenty ships under sail at the same time.

We had no lack for food while upon the island for if we did not wish to trouble our friends for a dinner, we only had to borrow a spade or a hoe and a kettle and go to the beach and dig a peck of clams. These, when boiled, would make a delicious meal which we often availed ourselves of.

One day, Elder Hale and I ascended to the top of a high granite rock upon the South Island for prayer and upplication.   We sat down under down under the shade of a pine tree which grew out of a fissure in the rock, and Elder Hale read the 16th chapter of Jeremiah, where mention is made of the hunters and fishers that God would send in the last days to gather Israel.

Of a truth, here we were upon an island of the sea, standing upon a rock where we could survey the gallant ships and also the islands which were as full of rocks, ledges and caves as any part of the earth. And what had brought us here? To search out the blood of Ephraim, the honest and meek of the earth, and gather them from those islands, rocks, holes and caves of the earth unto Zion.

We prayed, sang and rejoiced together. The Spirit of God rested upon us; we spoke of Christ and the ancient prophets and apostles in Jerusalem; of Nephi, Alma, Mormon and Moroni in America; Joseph, Hyrum, Oliver and the apostles in our own day, and we rejoiced that we were upon the islands of the sea searching out the blood of Israel.

While being filled with these meditations and the Spirit of God, we fell upon our knees and gave thanks to the God of heaven and felt to pray for all Israel.

After spending most of the day in praise and thanksgiving, we descended to the settlement and held a meeting with the people.

On the 6th of September, we called upon Captain Benjamin Coombs and visited his flakes, where he had one thousand quintals of codfish drying for the market. They had mostly been caught in the region of Newfoundland. While we were passing Carvey's Wharf our attention was called to a large school of mackerel playing by the side of the wharf. Several men were pitching them out with hooks. We also flung in a hook and caught all we wanted, then went on our way.

CHAPTER XII.

RETURN TO THE MAINLAND—PARTING WITH BROTHER HALE—MY SECOND VISIT TO THE ISLANDS—VISIT TO THE ISLE OF HOLT—A SIGN DEMANDED BY MR. DOUGLASS—A PREDICTION ABOUT HIM—ITS SUBSEQUENT FULFILLING—SPIRIT OF OPPOSITION—FIRING OFF CANNONS AND GUNS TO DISTURB MY MEETING.

WE continued to labor, preaching and baptizing and organized a branch of the Church upon each island and, finally on the 2nd of October, we parted from the Saints on the North Island to return to Scarboro for a short time.

We walked from Thomaston to Bath, a distance of forty-six miles, in one day and at the latter place attended a Baptist convention. I also preached there to a large congregation in the evening; the people gave good attention and wished to learn more about our doctrines.

On the day following, we walked thirty-six miles to Portland and the next day to Scarboro. Here I again met with my wife and her father's family.

The time had come for me to give the parting hand to Brother Jonathan H. Hale. We had traveled during the season over two thousand miles together with our hearts and spirits well united.

He felt it his duty to return to his family at Kirtland, but duty called me to return to my field of labor upon the islands.

On the 9th of October, I accompanied Brother Hale one mile upon his journey. We retired to a grove and knelt down and prayed together and had a good time and, after commending each other to God, we parted: he to return to Kirtland and I to the Fox Islands.

I spent fourteen days visiting the Saints and friends, and holding meetings among them, and on the 20th of October, I took leave of Father Carter and family and, in company with my wife, rode to Portland and spent the night with my brother-in-law, Ezra Carter.

A severe storm arose so we could not go to sea until November 1st, when we took a steamer to Owl's Head, a carriage to Thomaston and a sloop to Fox Islands.

My second visit to these islands was made under very different circumstances than the first. On my first visit, I was an entire stranger to the people, and they were strangers to the gospel; but upon my second I met many Saints who had received the gospel and who hailed me and my companion, with glad hearts.

On Sunday, the 5th of November, I met with a large assembly of Saints and friends, and again commenced baptizing such as would receive my testimony.

After visiting the North Island and holding meetings with the Saints there and baptizing two after meeting, I embarked on board a sloop with Captain Coombs for another island called the Isle of Holt. We arrived at noon and I preached to the people at night in their school-house and had an attentive audience. I spent the night with John Turner, Esq., who purchased a copy of the Book of Mormon.

On the following day, we returned to Fox Islands and as St. Paul once had to row hard to make the land in a storm, we had to row hard to make it in a calm.

After preaching on the North Island again and baptizing two persons at the close of the meeting, I returned again to the mainland in company with Mrs. Woodruff and others where I spent fifteen days, during which time I visited among the people, held twelve meetings, and baptized several persons. On the 13th of December, I returned again to the North Island where I held several meetings, and then crossed over to the South Island.

On the 20th of December, I spent an hour with Mr. Isaac Crockett in clearing away large blocks of ice from the water in a cove in order to baptize him, which I did when the tide came in. I also baptized two more in the same place on the 26th, and again two others on the 27th.

On the 28th, I held a meeting at a schoolhouse when William Douglass, the Methodist minister, came and wanted me to work a miracle that he might believe, and otherwise railed against me.

I told him what class of men asked for signs, and that he was a wicked and adulterous man, and predicted that the curse of God would rest upon him, and that his wickedness would be made manifest in the eyes of the people. (While visiting these islands several years afterwards, I learned that the prediction had really been fulfilled, and that he was serving out a fourteen years' term of imprisonment for a beastly crime).

Mrs. Woodruff crossed the thoroughfare in a boat and walked ten miles, the length of the island, to meet me on the last day of year. I held a meeting the same day in the school-house and at the close of the meeting baptized two persons in the sea at full tide before a large assembly.

January 1st, 1838, found me standing upon one of the islands of the sea, a minister of the gospel of life and salvation unto the people, laboring alone, though blessed with the society of Mrs. Woodruff, my companion. I had been declaring the word of the Lord through the islands many days; the Spirit of God was working among the people; prejudice was giving way; and the power of God was manifest by signs following those who believed.

I spent this New Year's Day visiting the Saints and their neighbors, and met a congregation at Captain Chas. Brown's where I spoke to them for awhile, and at the close of my remarks led three persons down into the sea and baptized them. Two of these were sea captains, namely, Charles Brown and Jesse Coombs, and the third was the wife of Captain Coombs. After confirming them, we spent the evening in preaching, singing and praying.

I held meetings almost daily with the Saints up to the 13th, when I crossed to the North Island. Here I found that the seed I had sown was bringing forth fruit. Six persons were ready for baptism.

But my mission upon these islands was not an exception to the general rule: success did not come without many obstacles presenting themselves. Those who rejected the word were frequently inspired by the evil one to make an attempt at persecution.

Some of those who felt to oppose me went down to the harbor and got a swivel and small arms and planted them close by the school-house near the sea shore, and while I was speaking they commenced firing their cannon and guns. I continued speaking in great plainness, but my voice was mingled with the report of musketry.

I told the people my garments were clear of the blood of the inhabitants of that island, and asked if any wished to embrace the gospel. Two persons came forward and wished to be baptized and I baptized them.

On the following day when I went down to the seaside to baptize a man, the rabble commenced firing guns again, as on the previous night. I afterwards learned that notices were posted up warning me to leave the town, but I thought it was better to obey God than man and, therefore, did not go.

The next day I baptized three persons, and two days subsequently a couple of others.

I had ample evidence of the fact that lying spirits had gone out into the world, for three persons whom I hadbaptized had been visited by

Mr. Douglass who told them that I denied the Bible and could not be depended upon; and they yielded to his insinuations until the devil took possession of them, and they were in a disaffected condition and sent for me.

When I met them they were in great affliction, but when I instructed them in regard to the principles of the gospel, and administered to them, they were delivered from the evil influence and rejoiced.

CHAPTER XIII.

MEETING WITH JAMES TOWNSEND—DECIDE TO GO TO BANGOR — A LONG JOURNEY THROUGH DEEP SNOW—CURIOUS PHENO-MENON — REFUSED LODGING AT EIGHT HOUSES—ENTERTAINED BY MR. TEPPLEY—CURIOUS COINCIDENCE -- MR. TEPPLEY'S DESPONDENCY — ARRIVAL AT BANGOR — RETURN TO THE ISLANDS — ADVENTURE WITH THE TIDE.

ON the 5th of February, I again crossed to the North Island and after remaining there seven days visiting, we returned to Camden. Here I met Brother James Townsend who had just arrived from Scarboro.

I ordained Brother Townsend to the office of an Elder and we concluded to take a journey to Bangor and offer the gospel to the inhabitants of that city.

We undertook the journey on foot in the dead of winter when the snow was very deep, and the first day broke the road for seven miles to Scarsmont. The day following, it being Sunday, we held two meetings, preached the gospel to the people, and were kindly entertained.

On the evening of the next day, we wallowed through snowdrifts for a mile to meet an appointment to preach in a school-house, and I got one of my ears frozen on the way; but notwithstanding the severity of the weather, we had quite a large and attentive audience. We also spent the next two days with the people there and held meetings.

On the evening of the 21st of February, as we came out of the school-house, a light appeared in the north-eastern horizon and spread to the west and soon rolled over our heads. It had the appearance of fire, blood and smoke, and at times resembled contending armies. The heavens were illuminated for the space of half an hour. It seemed at times as though the veil was about to rend in twain and the elements were contending with each other.

We looked upon it as one of the signs in the heavens predicted by the prophets of old as to appear in the last days. We were wading through deep snowdrifts most of the time while witnessing this remarkable scene.

The following day, we walked fifteen miles through deep snow to Belfast, and, after being refused lodging for the night by eight families, we were kindly entertained by a Mr. Thomas Teppley.

There was an interesting incident connected with our stay at his house. After eating our supper, it being late in the evening, Mr. Teppley placed a stand before me with a Bible upon it and asked me to read a chapter and have prayers with them, he being a religious man.

I opened the Bible mechanically, when—the 25th chapter of Matthew being the first to catch my eye—I read it, and as I closed the book Mr. Teppley turned to his wife and said, "Is not this a strange thing?" Then he explained to us that he had just read that chapter and closed the book when we rapped at the door, and he felt impressed to say, "Walk in, gentlemen." There is probably no other chapter in the whole book that would have the same influence in causing any one to feed a person who professed to be a servant of God, and asked for bread.

After becoming acquainted with his circumstances, I thought it providential that we we were led to his house, for although he was a professor of religion and a Methodist, he was in a state of despair believing that he had committed the unpardonable sin.

However, I told him what the unpardonable sin was, and that he had not committed it; but that it was a trick of the devil to make him think so in order to torment him. He then acknowledged that he went down to the wharf a few evenings before, with the intention of drowning himself, but when he looked into the cold, dark water he desisted and returned home, and had said nothing previously to anyone about it.

I taught him the principles of the gospel, which proved a comfort to him. We spent the following day in visiting the people of Belfast, and in the evening preached in a brick school-house, provided by Mr. Teppley, and many wished to hear more from us.

We next visited Northport and Frankfort, holding meetings at both places, and on the 1st of March, 1838, we entered Bangor, which at that time had a population of 10,000. This was my birthday, I being thirty-one years of age.

I visited some of the leading men of Bangor, and they granted me the use of the City Hall, where I preached to good audiences for two successive evenings. This was the first time a Latter-day Saint Elder had ever preached in that town. Many were anxious to learn more about our principles, but our visits through all the towns from Thomaston to Bangor were necessarily brief owing to our appointments upon the islands. It was like casting our bread upon the waters and trusting in God for the result.

On the 5th of March, we sailed from Penobscot for the Isle of Holt where I held a meeting on the following evening.

The next day I took passage on the mail boat for the North Island where I again had the privilege of meeting with the Saints for prayer and praise before the Lord.

On my arrival I received a package of letters from friends abroad. One was from Kirtland, and gave an account of the apostasy and tribulations which the Saints were passing through. Joseph, the prophet, and others, with their families, had gone to Far West and the Saints were following them.

Brother Townsend returned home and I was again left alone in the ministry.

On the afternoon of the 22nd of March, Brother Sterrett and I, accompanied by our wives, went several hundred yards from shore to a sand bar (it being low tide), to dig clams. The ground near shore was much lower than the bar we were on, and while we were all busy digging clams and talking "Mormonism," the dashing of the waves of the incoming tide against the shore suddenly made us conscious that we had fifty yards of water between us and the shore.

The surf waves also added to our difficulty, and as we had no boat, our only alternative was to cross our four arms, thus forming a kind of armchair for our wives to sit upon, and carry them in turn to shore wading through two-and-a-half feet of water.

By the time we got our wives and clams safely landed, the truth of the maxim was firmly impressed upon our minds, that "Time and tide wait for no man," not even for a preacher of the gospel.

CHAPTER XIV.

COUNSELED TO GATHER WITH THE SAINTS— REMARKABLE MANIFESTATION — CASE OF HEALING — EFFORTS OF APOSTATES — VISIT FROM ELDERS—A CONFERENCE—CLOSING MY LABORS ON THE ISLANDS FOR A SEASON.

ON the 28th of March, I received a letter from Zion requesting me to counsel the Saints I had baptized to sell their property and gather up to Zion.

About this time, the Lord was manifesting Himself upon the Islands in various ways: by dreams, visions, healings, signs and wonders. I will relate one peculiar circumstance of this kind that occurred.

Mr. Ebenezer Carver had been investigating our doctrines for quite a length of time, and, having a great desire to know the truth of our religion, he walked to the sea shore, wishing that he might have some manifestation in proof of its truth.

The passage of scripture came to his mind that there would be no sign given "but the sign of the prophet Jonas," and while this thought was in his mind a large fish arose to the top of the water a distance from him in the sea, and suddenly sank out of sight. He much desired to see it again, and soon it arose to the top of the water, accompanied by another fish of about the same size, and one of them swam on the water in a straight line towards Mr. Carver as he stood upon the shore. It came as near to him as the water would permit, and then stopped and gazed at him with a penetrating eye, as though it had a message for him. It then returned to its mate in the ocean and swam out of sight.

Mr. Carver retraced his steps homeward, meditating upon the scene and the wonderful condescension of the Lord.

It is proper to remark that this was at a season of the year when fish of that size are never known upon those shores or seas, and they are never, at any season, known to come ashore as in the case mentioned.

Mr. Carver was convinced that it was intended by the Lord as a sign to him.

Two days after this event, I visited Mr. Carver at his house and found his wife confined to her bed with a fever, and she requested me to administer to her. I placed my hands upon her head, the power of God rested upon me, and I commanded her in the name of Jesus Christ to arise and walk.

She arose and was healed from that instant, and she walked down to the sea and I baptized her in the same place where the fish visited her husband. I confirmed her there and she was filled with the Holy Ghost and returned to her home rejoicing.

I now called the people together and exhorted them to sell their property and prepare to accompany me to the land of Zion. I had labored hard for many days for the temporal and spiritual welfare of the inhabitants of those islands, and the Lord had blessed my labors and given me many souls as seals of my ministry for which I felt to praise Him; and now I felt to labor quite as zealously to gather out those who had embraced the gospel and lead them to Zion.

The worst difficulty which the Saints had to contend with in that day was from false brethren. Warren Parrish, who had been a prominent Elder in the Church and had labored with me as a missionary, had apostatized and been cut off from the Church. Learning that I was building up branches of the Church upon the island, he and other apostates conspired to block up my way by writing lies to the people and stirring up a spirit of mobocracy upon the islands.

They succeeded in exerting a strong influence with the wicked, but I knew they could not hinder the work of God.

On the 6th of April, I held a meeting at Brother Ebenezer Carver's and, though the hearts of the wicked were stirred up in bitterness against me, the Spirit of God was with me and at the close of the meeting, I baptized three persons. One of these was Mrs. Abigail Carver, the mother of Ebenezer Carver, who was seventy years of and in poor health. She had not so much as visited a neighbor's house for six years, but upon this occasion she walked with boldness to the sea shore and I baptized her, and she returned rejoicing.

On the 11th of April I had the happy privilege of again meeting with Elders Milton Holmes, James Townsend and Abner Rogers, who had come to the islands to attend conference with me.

We held our conference on the 13th of April on North Fox Island and had a representation of the different branches on the islands. We also preached and bore our testimony, ordained several and baptized one person at the close of the meeting.

On the 17th of April Mrs. Woodruff left the islands to return to her father's home in Scarboro, Maine, and a few days afterwards I called the Saints of the North Island together and communed with and instructed them. I also informed them that the Spirit of God bore record to me that it was our duty to leave the islands for a season and take a western mission. They had been faithfully warned and the Saints were established in the truth, while the wicked were contending against us, and some were disposed to take our lives they had the power.

CHAPTER XV.

RETURN TO SCARBORO—JOURNEY SOUTH — VISIT TO A. P. ROCKWOOD IN PRISON— INCIDENT OF PRISON LIFE — JOURNEY TO CONNECTICUT — BAPTIZE MY FATHER'S HOUSEHOLD.

ON the 28th of April, we left the island in an open sail boat and made our way to Owl's Head and then walked twenty miles. The following day we walked forty miles and suffered some with weary limbs and blistered feet, but we felt that it was for the gospel's sake and did not choose to complain. The next day a walk of thirty miles brought us to Scarboro where we spent the night at Father Carter's.

On the 8th of May, I parted with Mrs. Woodruff and Father Carter and family, and in company with Milton Holmes walked thirty-three miles towards Portsmouth, which city we reached the following day and spent several hours there visiting the navy yard. We then walked to Georgetown, formerly New Rowley, and spent the night with Father Nathaniel Holmes.

On the 11th of May, I visited Charleston and Bunker Hill monument, and also spent several hours in the city of Boston which then contained a population of 100,000. I ascended to the cupola of the court house from which I had a fine view of the city. I visited several of the Saints in the city and walked over the long bridge to Cambridge and Cambridgeport.

I visited the jail there in order to have an interview with Brother A. P. Rockwood, who had been cast into prison on the plea of debt in order to trouble and distress him because he was a "Mormon." This was the first time we had ever met.

The jailer permitted me to enter the room where he was. It was the first time in my life I had ever entered a prison. The jailer turned the key upon us and locked us both in.

I found Brother Rockwood strong in the faith of the gospel. He had the Bible, Book of Mormon, Voice of Warning and *Evening and Morning Star* as his companions, which he read daily.

We conversed together for three hours in this solitary abode. He informed me of many things which had transpired while he was confined there as a prisoner. Among other things, he mentioned that the jail had taken fire a few days previous to my visit. He said it looked a little like a dark hour. The fire was roaring over his head while uproar and confusion were upon every hand. Fire engines were rapidly playing around the building, with water pouring into every room. The people were hallooing in the streets. Prisoners were begging for mercy's sake to be let out or they would be consumed in the fire. One was struggling in the agonies of death, while others were cursing and swearing. Brother Rockwood said he felt composed in the midst of it until the fire was extinguished.

At eight o'clock the jailer unlocked the prison door to let me out, and I gave the parting hand to the prisoner of hope.

We had spent a pleasant time together and he rejoiced at my visit; and who would not be glad to meet with a friend in a lonely prison. I left him in good spirits and wended my way back to Boston.

I spent several days in Boston holding meetings with the Saints there, and then walked to Providence, Rhode Island, preaching by the way.

I there took a steamer and arrived in New York on the 18th of May, where I met with Elder Orson Pratt and his family, and Elijah Fordham and near one hundred Saints who had been baptized in the city of New York.

I spent three days in New York visiting the Saints and holding meetings. Several new converts were baptized while I was there.

Leaving New York, I traveled through New Jersey and returned to Farmington, Connecticut, the residence of my father. I arrived at his house on the 12th of June.

It was with peculiar sensations that I walked over my native land where I spent my youth and cast my eyes over the Farmington meadows and the hills and dales where I had roamed in my boyhood with my father, step-mother, brothers and half sister.

On my arrival at my father's home, I had the happy privilege of once more taking my parents and sister by the hand, also my uncle, Ozem Woodruff, who was among the number I had baptized the year before.

After spending an hour in conversation, we sat down around our father's table and supped together and were refreshed. Then we bowed upon our knees together in the family circle and offered up the gratitude of our hearts to God for preserving our lives and reuniting us.

I spent the next eighteen days in Farmington and Avon, visiting my father's household my uncles, aunts, cousins, neighbors and friends, preaching the gospel of Jesus Christ unto them and striving to bring them into the kingdom of God.

On the 1st of July, 1838, one of the most interesting events transpired of my whole life in the ministry. When Father Joseph Smith gave me my patriarchal blessing, among the many wonderful things of my life, he promised me that I should bring my father's household into the kingdom of God, and I felt that if I ever obtained the blessing the time had come for me to perform it.

By the help of God, I preached the gospel faithfully to my father's household and to all that were with him, as well as to my other relatives, and I had appointed a meeting on Sunday, the 1st of July, at my father's home.

My father was believing my testimony, as were all in his household, but upon this occasion the devil was determined to hinder the fulfillment of the promise of the patriarch unto me.

It seemed as though Lucifer, the son of the morning, had gathered together the hosts of hell and exerted his powers upon us all. Distress overwhelmed the whole household, and all were tempted to reject the work. And it seemed as though the same power would devour me. I had to take to my bed for an hour before the time of meeting. I there prayed unto the Lord with my whole soul for deliverance, for I knew the power of the devil was exercised to hinder me from accomplishing what God had promised me.

The Lord heard my prayer and answered my petition and when the hour of meeting came I arose from my bed and could sing and shout for joy to think I had been delivered from the power of the evil one.

Filled with the power of God, I stood up in the midst of the congregation and preached the gospel of Jesus Christ unto the people in great plainness.

At the close of the meeting, we assembled on the banks of the Farmington River, "because there was much water there," and I led six of my friends into the river and baptized them for the remission of their sins.

All of my father's household were included in this number, according to the promise of the patriarch. They were all relatives except Dwight Webster, who was a Methodist class-leader and was boarding with my father's family.

I organized the small number of nine persons, eight of whom were my relatives, into a branch of the Church, and ordained Dwight Webster to the office of a priest and administered the sacrament unto them.

It was truly a day of joy to my soul. My father, step-mother and sister were among the number baptized. I afterwards added a number of relatives. I felt that this day's work alone amply repaid me for all my labor in the ministry.

Who can comprehend the joy, the glory, the happiness and consolation that an Elder of Israel feels in being an instrument in the hands of God of bringing his father, mother, sister, brother, or any of the posterity of Adam through the door that enters into life and salvation? No man can, unless he has experienced these things and possesses the testimony of Jesus Christ and the inspiration of Almighty God.

CHAPTER XVI.

TAKING LEAVE OF MY OLD HOME—RETURN TO MAINE—BIRTH OF MY FIRST CHILD—APPOINTMENT TO THE APOSTLESHIP AND TO A FOREIGN MISSION—PREPARATION FOR THE JOURNEY TO ZION.

NOW, as my mission to my native land was accomplished, which I felt impressed to take while upon the islands, I felt it my duty to return there.

Monday, July 2nd, 1838, was the last day and night I spent at my father's home while upon this mission. At the setting of the sun I took the last walk with my sister I ever had with her while in my native State. We walked by the canal and viewed the river and fields, and conversed upon our future destiny.

After evening prayer with the family, my father retired to rest, and I spent a season with my step-mother who had reared me from my infancy. In conversation we felt sensibly the weight of the power of temptation, out of which the Lord had delivered us.

I also spent a short time with my sister Eunice, the only sister I was ever blessed with in my father's family. I had baptized her into the Church and Kingdom of God and we mingled our sympathies, prayers and tears together before the throne of grace.

How truly are the bonds of consanguinity and of the blood of Christ united in binding the hearts of the Saints of God together, and "how blessings brighten as they take their flight!"

This being the last night I was to spend beneath my father's roof while upon this mission, I felt the weight of it and my prayer was, "O Lord, protect my father's house and bring him to Zion!" (Which prayer was granted.)

On the morning of July 3rd, I took leave of my relatives and my native land and started on my return to Maine. I arrived in Scarboro on the 6th, and on the 14th my first child, a daughter, was born at Father Carter's house. We named her Sarah Emma.

On the 30th of July, I left my wife and child at Father Carter's and started once more to visit Fox Islands.

While holding meeting with the Saints at North Vinal Haven on the 9th of August, I received a letter from Thomas B. Marsh who was then President of the Twelve Apostles, informing me that Joseph Smith, the Prophet, had received a revelation naming as persons to be chosen to fill the places of those who had fallen: John E. Page, John Taylor, Wilford Woodruff and Willard Richards.

President Marsh added in his letter, "Know then, Brother Woodruff, by this, that you are appointed to fill the place of one of the Twelve Apostles, and that it is agreeable to the word of the Lord, given very lately, that you should come speedily to Far West, and, on the 26th of April next, take your leave of the Saints here and depart for other climes across the mighty deep."

The substance of this letter had been revealed to me several weeks before, but I had not named it to any person.

The time having now come for me to prepare for leaving the islands, I had a desire to take with me all the Saints I could get to go to Zion. There had already been a line drawn upon the islands between the Saints and those who had rejected the gospel, and the enemies were very bitter against me and the work of God that I had labored to establish. They threatened my life, but the Saints were willing to stand by me.

I spent four days with the Saints visiting them, holding meetings and encouraging them, while the devil was raging upon every hand.

I had baptized and organized into the Church nearly one hundred persons while upon the islands, and there seemed prospect of gathering about half of them with me, but the devil raged to such an extent that quite a number were terrified.

The inhabitants of the islands had but little acquaintance with the management of horses or wagons; in fact, most of them knew more about handling a shark than a horse. However, in company with Nathaniel Thomas, who had sold his property and had money, I went to the mainland and purchased ten new wagons, ten sets of harness and twenty horses. When I got every-thing prepared for the company to start, I left the affairs with Brother Thomas, and went on ahead of the company to Scarboro to prepare my family for the journey.

family for the journey.

The outfit which I purchased for the company cost about $2,000.00.

Before leaving Brother Thomas, I counseled him in regard to the courage to pursue, and charged him not to be later than the 1st of September in starting from the mainland.

I arrived at Father Carter's on the 19th of August, and waited with great anxiety for the arrival of the company from the islands, but instead of reaching there by the 1st of September, they did not arrive till the 3rd of October; and when they did arrive the wagon covers were all flying in the breeze. It took a good day's work to nail down the covers, paint the wagons and get prepared for the journey.

CHAPTER XVII.

START UPON JOURNEY—A HAZARDOUS UNDERTAKING — SICKNESS — SEVERE WEATHER—MY WIFE AND CHILD STRICKEN— A TRYING EXPERIENCE — MY WIFE CONTI- NUES TO FAIL—HER SPIRIT LEAVES HER BODY—RESTORED BY THE POWER OF GOD— HER SPIRIT'S EXPERIENCE WHILE SEPA- RATED FROM THE BODY—DEATH OF MY BROTHER—ARRIVAL AT ROCHESTER—RE- MOVAL TO QUINCY

ON the afternoon of the 9th of October, we took leave of Father Carter and family and started upon our journey of 2,000 miles at this late season of the year, taking my wife with a suckling babe at her breast with me to lead a company of fifty-three souls from Maine to Illinois, and to spend nearly three months in traveling in wagons through rain, mud, snow and frost. It was such a trial as I never before had attempted during my experience as a minister of the gospel.

On our arrival at Georgetown we were joined by Elder Milton Holmes. We traveled each day as far as we could go and camped wherever night overtook us.

On the 13th of October, while crossing the Green Mountains, I was attacked with something resembling the cholera. I was very sick. I stopped at a house for about two hours but the Elders administered to me, and I revived.

On the 24th, I was again taken sick and my wife and child were also stricken down. We also had several others sick in the company through the exposure of the journey.

On the 31st we had our first snow storm and the horses dragged our wagons all day through mud, snow and water.

On the 2nd of November, Elder Milton Holmes left us and took a steamer for Fairport, and two days afterwards, a little boy of Nathaniel Holmes', about six years of age, died and we had to bury him at Westfield.

The roads finally became so bad and the cold so severe that Nathaniel Thomas and James Townsend concluded to stop for the winter. We parted with them on the 21st of November, near New Portage, Ohio.

On the 23rd of November, my wife, Phoebe, was attacked with a severe headache, which terminated in brain fever. She grew more and more distressed daily as we continued our journey. It was a terrible ordeal for a woman to travel in a wagon over rough roads, afflicted as she was. At the same time our child was also very sick.

The 1st of December was a trying day to any soul. My wife continued to fail and in the afternoon, about 4 o'clock, she appeared to be struck with death. I stopped my team, and it seemed as though she would breath her last lying in the wagon. Two of the sisters sat beside her, to see if they could do anything for her in her last moments.

I stood upon the ground in deep affliction and meditated. I cried unto the Lord and prayed that she might live and not be taken from me. I claimed the promises the Lord had made unto me through the prophets and patriarchs, and soon her spirit revived, and I drove a short distance to a tavern and got her into a room and worked over her and her babe all night, and prayed to the Lord to preserve her life.

In the morning, the circumstances were such that I was under the necessity of removing my wife from the inn, as there was so much noise and confusion at the place that she could not endure it. I carried her out to her bed in the wagon and drove two miles, when I alighted at a house and carried my wife and her bed into it with a determination to tarry there until she either recovered her health or passed away.   This was on Sunday morning, December 2nd.

After getting my wife and things into the house and wood provided to keep up a fire, I employed my time in taking care of her. It looked as though she had but a short time to live.

She called me to her bedside in the evening and said she felt as though a few moments more would end her existence in this life. She manifested great confidence in the cause she had embraced, and exhorted me to have confidence in God and to keep His commandments.

To all appearances, she was dying. I laid hands upon her and prayed for her and she soon revived and slept some during the night.

December 3rd found my wife very low. I spent the day in taking care of her, and the following day I returned to Eaton to get some things for her. She seemed to be gradually sinking, and in the evening her spirit apparently left her body and she was dead.

The sisters gathered around her body weeping, while I stood looking at her in sorrow. The spirit and power of God began to rest upon me until, for the first time during her sickness, faith filled my soul—although she lay before me as one dead.

I had some oil that was consecrated for my anointing while in Kirtland. I took it and consecrated it again before the Lord for anointing the sick. I then bowed down before the Lord and prayed for the life of my companion, and I anointed her body with the oil in the name of the Lord. I laid my hands upon her, and in the name of Jesus Christ I rebuked the power of death and the destroyer, and commanded the same to depart from her and the spirit of life to enter her body.

Her spirit returned to her body and from that hour she was made whole; and we all felt to praise the name of God and to trust in Him and to keep His commandments.

While this operation was going on with me (as my wife related afterwards) her spirit left her body, and she saw her body lying upon the bed, and the sisters weeping. She looked at them and at me and upon her babe and, while gazing upon this scene, two personages came into the room carrying a coffin and told her they had come for her body. One of these messengers informed her that she could have her choice: she might go to rest in the spirit world, or on one condition, she could have the privilege of returning to her tabernacle and continuing her labors upon the earth. The condition was, if she felt that she could stand by her husband, and with him pass through all the cares, trials, tribulations and afflictions of life which he would be called to pass through for the gospel's sake unto the end. When she looked at the situation of her husband and child she said: "Yes, I will do it!"

At the moment that decision was made, the power of faith rested upon me and when I administered unto her, her spirit entered her tabernacle, and she saw the messengers carry the coffin out at the door.

On the morning of the 6th of December, the Spirit said to me: "Arise, and continue thy journey!" and through the mercy of God my wife was enabled to arise and dress herself and walk to the wagon, and we went on our way rejoicing.

On the night of the 11th I stopped for the night at an inn, the weather being very cold. I there learned of the sudden death of my brother, Asahel H. Woodruff, a merchant of Terre Haute, Ind.

I had anticipated a joyful meeting with this brother on the following day. Instead of this, I only had the privilege of visiting his grave, in company with my wife, and examining a little into his business.

I was offered the position of administrator of his affairs, but I was leading a company of Saints to Zion, and could not stop to attend to his temporal business. Strangers settled his affairs and took possession of his property. His relatives obtained nothing from his effects except a few trifling mementos.

I left this place and crossed into Illinois on the 13th of December, and arrived at Rochester on the 19th and, getting information of the severe persecutions of the Saints in Missouri and the unsettled state of the Church at that time, we concluded to stop at Rochester and spend the winter.

Thus ended my journey of two months and sixteen days, leading the Fox Island Saints to the west, through all the perils of a journey of nearly two thousand miles, in the midst of sickness and great severity of weather.

I took my family in the spring and removed to Quincy, Illinois, where I could mingle with my brethren, and I felt to praise God for His protecting care over me and my family in all our afflictions.

CHAPTER XVIII.

A PECULIAR REVELATION—DETERMINATION OF ENEMIES TO PREVENT ITS FULFILLMENT—START TO FAR WEST TO FULFILL THE REVELATION—OUR ARRIVAL THERE—HOLD A COUNCIL—FULFILL THE REVELATION--CORNERSTONE OF THE TEMPLE LAID—ORDAINED TO THE APOSTLESHIP—LEAVE FAR WEST—MEET THE PROPHET JOSEPH — A CONFERENCE HELD—SETTLE OUR FAMILIES IN NAUVOO.

JOSEPH SMITH, the Prophet, asked the Lord what His will was concerning the Twelve, and the Lord answered in a revelation given July 8th, 1838, in which He says: "Let them take leave of my Saints in the city Far West, on the 26th day of April next, on the building spot of my house, saith the Lord. Let my servant John Taylor, and also my servant John E. Page, and also my servant Wilford Woodruff, and also my servant Willard Richards, be appointed to fill the places of those who have fallen, and be officially notified of their appointment."

It will be observed that this differs from nearly all other revelations in this respect, a fixed day and stated place were given for the commencement of the mission. When the revela-

-tion was given, all was peace and quietude in Far West, Missouri, the city where most of the Latter-day Saints dwelt; but before the time came for its fulfillment, the Saints of God had been driven out of the State of Missouri into the State of Illinois under the edict of Governor Boggs; and the Missourians had sworn that if all the other revelations of Joseph Smith were fulfilled, that should not be. It stated the day and the place where the Twelve Apostles should take leave of the Saints to go on their mission across the great waters and the mobocrats of Missouri had declared that they would see that it should not be fulfilled.

It seemed as though the Lord, having a foreknowledge of what would take place, gave the revelation in this manner to see whether the Apostles would obey it at the risk of their lives.

When the time drew near for the fulfillment of this commandment of the Lord, Brigham Young was the President of the Twelve Apostles; Thos. B. Marsh who was the senior Apostle had fallen. Brother Brigham called together those of the Twelve who were then at Quincy, Illinois, to see what their minds would be about going to Far West to fulfill the revelation. The Prophet Joseph and his brother Hyrum, Sidney Rigdon, Lyman Wight and Parley P. Pratt were in prison in Missouri at that time; but Father Joseph Smith, the Patriarch, the Patriarch, was at Quincy, Illinois.   He and others who were present did not think it wisdom for us to attempt the journey, as our lives would be in great jeopardy. They thought the Lord would take the will for the deed. But when President Young asked the Twelve what our feelings were upon the subject, we all of us, as the voice of one man, said the Lord God had spoken and it was for us to obey. It was the Lord's business to take care of His servants, and we would fulfill the commandment, or die trying.

To fully understand the risk the Twelve Apostles ran in making this journey, my readers should remember that Lilburn W. Boggs, governor of the State of Missouri, had issued a proclamation in which all the Latter-day Saints were required to leave that State or be exterminated. Far West had been captured by the militia, who were really only an organized mob; the citizens had been compelled to give up their arms; all the leading men who could be got hold of had been taken prisoners; the rest of the Saints—men, women and children—had to flee as best they could out of the State to save their lives, leaving all their houses, lands and other property which they could not carry with them, to be taken by the mob. In fact, they shot down the cattle and hogs of the Saints wherever they could find them, and robbed them of nearly everything they could lay their hands upon.

Latter-day Saints were treated with merciless cruelty and had to endure the most outrageous abuses. It was with the greatest difficulty that many of them got out of the State, especially the prominent men; for there were many men of that State at that time who acted as though they thought it no more harm "to shoot a "Mormon" than a mad dog. From this brief explanation, you will be able to understand why some of the brethren thought we were not required to go back to Far West to start from there upon our mission across the ocean to Europe.

Having determined to carry out the require-ment of the revelation, on the 18th of April, 1839, I took into my wagon Brigham Young and Orson Pratt; and Father Cutler took into his wagon John Taylor and George A. Smith, and we started for Far West.

On the way we met John E. Page who was going with his family to Quincy, Illinois. His wagon had turned over and when we met him he was trying to gather up a barrel of soft soap with his hands. We helped him get up his wagon. He drove down into the valley below, left his wagon, and accompanied us on our way.

On the night of the 25th of April, we ar-rived at Far West and spent the night at the home of Morris Phelps (who was not there, however,) having been taken prisoner by the mob, was still in prison.

On the morning of the 26th of April, 1839, notwithstanding the threats of our enemies that the revelation which was to be fulfilled this day should not be, and notwithstanding that ten thousand of the Saints had been driven out of the State by the edict of the governor, and though the Prophet Joseph and his brother, Hyrum Smith, with other leading men were in the hands of our enemies in chains and in prison, we moved on to the temple grounds in the city of Far West and held a council and fulfilled the revelation and commandment given unto us, and we performed many other things at this council.

We excommunicated from the Church thirty -one persons who had apostatized and become its enemies.

The "Mission of the Twelve" was sung, and we then repaired to the south-east corner of the temple ground, and, with the assistance of Elder Alpheus Cutler, the Master workman of the building committee, laid the south-east chief corner stone of the temple, according to revelation.

There were present of the Twelve Apostles: Brigham Young, Heber C. Kimball, Orson Pratt, John E. Page and John Taylor, who proceeded to ordain Wilford Woodruff and Geo. A. Smith to the apostleship, and as members of the quorum of the Twelve in the places of those who had fallen as they had been called by revelation.

Darwin Chase and Norman Shearer, who had just been liberated from Richmond prison, were also ordained to the office of Seventies. The Twelve then offered up vocal prayer in the following order: Brigham Young, Heber C. Kimball, Orson Pratt, John E. Page, John Taylor, Wilford Woodruff and George A. Smith, after which we sang "Adam-ondi-Ahman."

The Twelve then took their leave of, and gave the parting hand to, the following Saints, agreeable to revelation: A. Butler, Elias Smith, Norman Shearer, Wm. Burton, Stephen Markham, Shadrach Roundy, Wm. O. Clark, John W. Clark, Hezekiah Peck, Darwin Chase, Richard Howard, Mary Ann Peck, Artimesia Granger, Martha Peck, Sarah Granger, Theodore Turley, Hiram Clark, and Daniel Shearer.

Bidding good-by to the small remnant of Saints who remained on the temple ground to see us fulfill the revelation and commandments of God, we turned our backs on Far West and Mis-souri and returned to Illinois. We had completed the mission without a dog moving his tongue at us or any man saying "Why do you so?"

We crossed the Mississippi River on the steam ferry, entered Quincy on the 2nd May, and all had the joy of reaching our families once more in peace and safety.

There was an incident connected with our journey that is worthy of record. While we were on our way to fulfill the revelation, Joseph, the Prophet, and his companions, in chains, had been liberated through the blessing of God from their enemies and prison, and they passed us. We were not far distant from each other but neither party knew it. They were making their way to their families in Illinois, while we were traveling to Far West into the midst of our enemies. So they came home to their families and friends before our return.

May 3rd was a very interesting day to me, as well as to others. In company with five others of the quorum of the Twelve, I rode four miles out of town to Mr. Cleveland's to visit Brother Joseph Smith and his family.

Once more I had the happy privilege of taking Brother Joseph by the hand. Two years had rolled away since I had seen his face. He greeted us with great joy, as did Hyrum Smith and Lyman Wight—all of whom had escaped from their imprisonment together. They had been con-fined in prison six months, and had been under sentence of death three times; yet their lives were in the hands of God and He had delivered them, and they were now mingling with their wives, children and friends, and out of the reach of the mob. Joseph was frank, open and familiar as usual, and our rejoicing was great.

No man can understand the joyful sensations created by such a meeting, except those who have been in tribulation for the gospel's sake. After spending the day together, we re-turned to our families at night.

On the day following, May 4th, we met in conference at Quincy, the Prophet Joseph presiding, which caused great joy and rejoicing to all the Saints.

On Sunday, May 5th, Joseph Smith addressed the assembly, followed by Sidney Rigdon and the Twelve Apostles. The Spirit of the Lord was poured out upon us and we had a glorious day.

On May 6th, I met with the Seventies and we ordained sixty men into the quorums of Elders and Seventies. Brother Joseph met with the Twelve, Bishops and Elders, at Bishop Partridge's house; and there were a, number with us who were wounded at Haun's Mill. Among them was Isaac Laney who had been in company with about twenty others at the mill when a large armed mob fired among them with rifles and other weapons and shot down seventeen of the brethren, and wounded more. Brother Laney fled from the scene, but they poured a shower of lead after him which pierced his body through and through. He showed me eleven bullet holes in his body. There were twenty-seven in his shirt, seven in his pantaloons, and his coat was literally cut to pieces. One ball entered one arm-pit and came out at the other.

Another entered his back and came out at the breast. A ball passed through each hip, each leg and each arm. All these shots were received while he was running for life, and, strange as it may appear, though he had also one of his ribs broken, he was able to outrun his enemies and his life was saved. We can only acknowledge this deliverance to be by the power and mercy of God.

President Joseph Young was also among the number. He also fled, and although the balls flew around him like hail, he was not wounded. How mysterious are the ways of the Lord!

Before starting on our missions to England, we were under the necessity of settling our families. A place called Commerce, afterwards named Nauvoo, was selected as the place at which our people should settle.

I left Quincy in company with Brother Brigham Young and our families on the 15th of May, and arrived in Commerce on the 18th. After an interview with Joseph we crossed the river at Montrose, Iowa. President Brigham Young and myself, with our families, occupied one room about fourteen feet square. Finally, Brother Young obtained another room and moved into it by himself. Then Brother Orson Pratt and family moved into the same room with myself and family.

CHAPTER XIX.

A DAY OF GOD'S POWER WITH THE PROPHET JOSEPH SMITH—A GREAT NUMBER OF SICK PERSONS HEALED—THE MOB BECOMES ALARMED—THEY TRY TO INTERFERE WITH THE HEALING OF THE SICK—THE MOB SENT OUT OF THE HOUSE—TWIN CHILDREN HEALED.

WHILE I was living in this cabin in the old barracks, we experienced a day of God's power with the Prophet Joseph. It was a very sickly time and Joseph had given up his home in Commerce to the sick and had a tent pitched in his door-yard and was living in that himself. The large number of Saints who had been driven out of Missouri were flocking into Commerce; but had no homes to go into and were living in wagons, in tents, and on the ground. Many, therefore, were sick through the exposure they were sub-jected to. Brother Joseph had waited on the sick, until he was worn out and nearly sick himself.

On the morning of the 22nd of July, 1839, he arose reflecting upon the situation of the Saints of God in their persecutions and afflictions, and he called upon the Lord in prayer and the power of God rested upon him mightily, and as Jesus healed all the sick around him in his day, so

Joseph, the Prophet of God, healed all around on this occasion. He healed all in his house and dooryard, then, in company with Sidney Rigdon and several of the Twelve, he went through among the sick lying on the bank of the river and he commanded them in a loud voice, in the name of Jesus Christ, to come up and be made whole, and they were all healed. When he had healed all that were sick on the east side of the river, they crossed the Mississippi River in a ferry boat to the west aide, to Montrose where we were. The first house they went into was President Brigham Young's. He was sick on his bed at the time. The Prophet went into his house and healed him; and they all came out together. As they were passing by my door, Brother Joseph said; "Brother Woodruff, follow me." These were the only words spoken by any of the company from the time they left Brother Brigham's house till we crossed the public square and entered Brother Fordham's house. Brother Fordham had been dying for an hour and we expected each minute would be his last.

I felt the power of God that was overwhelming His Prophet.

When we entered the house, Brother Joseph walked up to Brother Fordham and took him by the right hand; in his left hand he held his hat.

He saw that Brother Fordham's eyes were glazed, and that he was speechless and unconscious.

After taking hold of his hand, he looked down into the dying man's face and said: "Brother Fordham, do you not know me?" At first he made no reply; but we could all see the effect of the Spirit of God resting upon him.

He again said: "Elijah, do you not know me?"

With a low whisper, Brother Fordham answered, "yes!"

The Prophet then said, "Have you not faith to be healed?"

The answer, which was a little plainer than before, was: "I am afraid it is too late. If you had come sooner, I think it might have been."

He had the appearance of a man awaking from sleep. It was the sleep of death.

Joseph then said: "Do you not believe that Jesus is the Christ?"

"I do, Brother Joseph," was the response.

Then the Prophet of God spoke with a, loud voice, as in the majesty of the Godhead: "Elijah, I command you, in the name of Jesus of Nazareth, to arise and be made whole!"

The words of the Prophet were not like the words of man, but like the voice of God. It seemed to me that the house shook from its foundation.

Elijah Fordham leaped from his bed like a man raised from the dead. A healthy color came to his face, and life was manifest in every act. His feet were done up in Indian meal poultices. He kicked them off his feet, scattering the contents, and then called for his clothes and put them on. He asked for a bowl of bread and milk and ate it; then put on his hat and followed us into the street to visit others who were sick.

The unbeliever may ask: "Was there not deception in this?"

If there is any deception in the mind of the unbeliever, there was certainly none with Elijah Fordham, the dying man, nor with those who were present with him, for in a few minutes more he would have been in the spirit world had he not been rescued. Through the blessing of God, he lived up till 1880, in which year he died in Utah while all who were with him on that occasion, with the exception of two, are in the spirit world.

Among the number were Joseph and Hyrum Smith, Sidney Rigdon, Brigham Young, Heber C. Kimball, George A. Smith and Parley P. Pratt. Orson Pratt and Wilford Woodruff are the only two living who were present at the time, and we shall soon mingle with those that have gone.

As soon as we left Brother Fordham's house, we went into the house of Joseph B. Noble, who was very low and dangerously sick.

When we entered the house, Brother Joseph took him by the hand and commanded him in the name of Jesus Christ to arise and be made whole. He did arise and was immediately healed.

While this was going on, the wicked mob in the place, led by one Kilburn, had become alarmed, and followed us into Brother Noble's house.

Before they arrived there, Brother Joseph had called upon Brother Fordham to offer prayer.

While he was praying the mob entered, with all the evil spirits accompanying them.

As soon as they entered, Brother Fordham, who was praying, fainted and sank to the floor. When Joseph saw the mob in the house, he arose and had the room cleared of both that class of men and their attendant devils. Then Brother Fordham immediately revived and finished his prayer.

This shows what power evil spirits have upon the tabernacles of men. The Saints are only saved from the power of the devil by the power of God.

This case of Brother Noble's was the last one of healing upon that day. It was the greatest day for the manifestation of the power of God through the gift of healing since the organization of the Church.

When we left Brother Noble, Joseph went with those who accompanied him from the other side to the banks of the river to return home. While waiting for the ferry-boat, a man of the world, knowing of the miracles which had been performed, came to him and asked him if he would not go and heal two twin children of his, about five months old, who were both lying sick nigh unto death.

They were some two miles from Montrose.

The Prophet said he could not go; but, after pausing some time, he said he would send some one to heal them; and he turned to me and said: "You go with the man and heal his children."

He took a red silk handkerchief out of his pocket and gave it to me, and told me to wipe their faces with the handkerchief when I administered to them, and they should be healed. He also said unto me: "As long as you will keep that handkerchief, it shall remain a league between you and me."

I went with the man and did as the Prophet commanded me, and the children were healed. I have possession of the handkerchief unto this day.

CHAPTER XX.

PREPARING FOR OUR MISSION—THE BLESSING OF THE PROPHET JOSEPH UPON OUR HEADS, AND HIS PROMISES UNTO US— THE POWER OF THE DEVIL MANIFESTED TO HINDER US IN THE PERFORMANCE OF OUR JOURNEY.

On the first of July, 1839, Joseph Smith and his counselors Sidney Rigdon and Hyrum Smith, crossed the river to Montrose to spend the day with the Twelve, and set them apart and bless them, before they started upon their missions. There were twelve of us who met there, and we all dined in my house.

After dinner, we assembled at Brother Brigham Young's house for our meeting.

Brother Hyrum Smith opened by prayer; after which the Presidency laid their hands upon our heads and gave each of us a blessing.

President Rigdon was mouth in blessing me, and also blessed Sisters Young, Taylor and Woodruff.

The Prophet Joseph promised us if we would be faithful, we should be blessed upon our mission, have many souls as seals of our ministry, and return again in peace and safety to our families and friends; all of which was fulfilled.

Brother Hyrum advised me to preach the first principles of the gospel; he thought that was about as much as this generation could endure. Then Joseph arose and preached some precious things of the Kingdom of God unto us, in the power of the Holy Ghost; some of which I here copy from my journal:

"Ever keep in exercise the principle of mercy, and be ready to forgive our brethren on the first intimation of their repentance and desire for forgiveness; for our Heavenly Father will be equally merciful unto us. We also ought to be willing to repent of and confess our sins, and keep nothing back. Let the Twelve be humble and not be exalted, and beware of pride and not seek to excel one another, but act for each other's good, and honorably make mention of each other's names in prayer before the Lord and before our fellow men. Do not backbite or devour a brother. The Elders of Israel should seek to learn by pre-cept and example in this late age of the world and not be obliged to learn everything we know by sad experience. I trust the remainder of the Twelve will learn wisdom and not follow the example of those who have fallen. When the Twelve or any other witnesses of Jesus Christ, stand before the congregations of the earth, and they preach in the power and demonstration of the Holy Ghost, and the people are astonished and confounded at the doctrine and say "That man has preached a powerful sermon," then let that man or those men take care that they do not ascribe the glory unto themselves, but be careful that they are humble and ascribe the glory to God and the Lamb; for it is by the power of the Holy Priesthood and the Holy Ghost that they have power thus to speak.

"Who art thou, O man, but dust! and from whom dost thou receive thy power and blessing, but from God?

"Then let the Twelve Apostles and Elders of Israel observe this key, and be wise: *Ye are not sent out to be taught, but to teach.*

"Let every man be sober, be vigilant, and let all his words be seasoned with grace, and keep in mind it is a day of warning, and not of many words.

"Act honestly before God and man; beware of sophistry, such as bowing and scraping unto men in whom you have no confidence. Be honest, open, and frank in all your intercourse with mankind.

"I wish to say to the Twelve and all the Saints, to profit by this important key, that in all your trials, troubles, temptations, afflictions, bonds, imprisonments and deaths, see to it that you do not betray Jesus Christ, that you do not betray the revelations of God, whether in the Bible, Book of Mormon, or Doctrine and Covenants, or any of the words of God.

"Yea, in all your troubles, see that you do not this thing, lest innocent blood be found upon your skirts, and ye go down to hell.

"We may ever know by this sign that there is danger of our being led to a fall and apostasy when we give way to the devil, so as to neglect the first known duty; but whatever you do, do not betray your friend."

The foregoing are some of the instructions given to the Twelve by the Prophet Joseph, before they started upon their missions.

Inasmuch as the devil had been in a measure thwarted by the Twelve going to Far West, and returning without harm, it seemed as though the destroyer was determined to make some other attempt upon us to hinder us from performing our mission; for it seemed that as soon as any one of the Apostles began to prepare for starting, he was smitten with chills and fever or sickness of some kind.

Nearly all of the quorum of the Twelve or their families began to be sick, so it still required the exercise of a good deal of faith and perseverance to start off on a mission.

On the 25th of July, for the first time in my life, I was attacked with chills and fever; and this I had every other day, and, whenever attacked, I was laid prostrate. My wife, Phoebe, was also soon taken down with chills and fever, as were quite a number of the Twelve.

I passed thirteen days in Montrose with my family after I was taken sick before I started on my mission.

The 7th of August was the last day I spent at home in Montrose, and although sick with the chills and fever the most of the day, I made what preparations I could to start on the morrow on a mission of four thousand miles to preach the gospel to the nations of the earth, and this, too, without purse or scrip, with disease resting upon me, and a stroke of fever and ague once every two days.

Yet I did this freely for Christ's sake, trusting in Him for the recompense or reward. My prayer was: "May the Lord give me grace according to my day and souls for my hire, and a safe return to my family and friends, which favor I ask in the name of Jesus Christ. Amen."

CHAPTER XXI.

LEAVING MY FAMILY — START UPON MY MISSION — OUR POOR CONDITION — ELDER TAYLOR THE ONLY ONE NOT SICK—REPROOF FROM THE PROPHET — INCIDENTS ON THE JOURNEY — ELDER TAYLOR STRICKEN — I LEAVE HIM SICK.

EARLY upon the morning of the 8th of August, I arose from my bed of sickness, laid my hands upon the head of my sick wife, Phoebe, and blessed her. I then departed from the embrace of my companion, and left her almost without food or the necessaries of life.

She parted from me with the fortitude that becomes a Saint, realizing the responsibilities of her companion. I quote from my journal:

"Phoebe, farewell! Be of good cheer; remember me in your prayers. I leave these pages for your perusal when I am gone. I shall see thy face again in the flesh. I go to obey the commands of Jesus Christ."

Although feeble, I walked to the banks of the Mississippi River. There President Brigham Young took me in a canoe (having no other conveyance) and paddled me across the river.

When we landed, I lay down on a side of sole leather by the post office to rest.

Brother Joseph, the Prophet of God, came along and looked at me.

"Well Brother Woodruff," said he, "you have started upon your mission."

Yes," said I, "but I feel and look more like a subject for the dissecting room than a missionary."

Joseph replied: "What did you say that for? Get up and go along; all will be right with you!"

I name these incidents that the reader may know how the quorum of the Twelve Apostles started on their missions to England in 1839.

Elder John Taylor was going with me, and we were the first two of the quorum of the Twelve who started on the mission.

Brother Taylor was about the only man in the quorum that was not sick.

Soon a brother came along with a wagon and took us in. As we were driving through the place, we came to Parley P. Pratt, who was stripped to the shirt and pants, with his head and feet bare. He was hewing a log, preparing to build a cabin.

He said: "Brother Woodruff, I have no money, but I have an empty purse which I will give you." He brought it to me, and I thanked him for it. We went a few rods further, and met Brother Heber C. Kimball, in the same condition, also hewing a log towards building a cabin.

He said : "As Parley has given you a purse, I have got a dollar I will give you to put in it." He gave me both a dollar and a blessing.

We drove sixteen miles across a prairie and spent the night with a Brother Merrill. The day following we rode ten miles to a Brother Perkins, and he took us in his wagon to Macomb, and from thence to Brother Don Carlos Smith's.

I rode four hours during the day over a very rough road of stones and stumps, lying on my back in the bottom of the wagon, shaking with the ague, and I suffered much.

We held a meeting in a grove near Don Carlos Smith's, and here Elder Taylor baptized George Miller, who afterwards was ordained a Bishop.

At the meeting, the Saints gave us nine dollars, and George Miller gave us a horse to help us on our journey.

I rode to Rochester with Father Coltrin, where I had an interview with several families of the Fox Island Saints, whom I had brought up with me from Fox Island in 1838. I spent several days with them and at Springfield, where Elder Taylor published fifteen hundred copies, in pamphlet form, of a brief sketch of the persecutions and sufferings of the Latter-day Saints inflicted by the inhabitants of Missouri.

We sold our horse, and in company with Father Coltrin, Brother Taylor and myself left Springfield, and continued our journey.

I had the chills and fever nearly every other day, which made riding in a lumber wagon very distressing to me, especially when I shook with the ague.

On the 24th of August, we rode to Terre Haute, and spent the night with Dr. Modisett. I suffered much with the chills and fever.

Elder John Taylor, up to this time, had appeared to enjoy excellent health, but the destroyer did not intend to make him an exception to the rest of the Apostles. On the 28th of August, he fell to the ground as though he had been knocked down. He fainted away but soon revived. On the following day, however, the enemy made a powerful attack on his life. He fainted away several times, and it seemed as though he would die. We stopped several hours with him at a house by the wayside. We then took him into the wagon and drove to Horace S. Eldredge's, and spent the remainder of the day and night doc-toring him.

In the morning, Brother Taylor was so far recovered that he thought he would be able to ride. So we started on our journey on the morning of the 30th, and we traveled forty miles, to Louisville and spent the night with the family of Brother James

Townsend.

We felt terribly shaken up, being in such a weak state. Brother Townsend was away from home, but we were kindly entertained by Sister Townsend.

In the morning, Elder Taylor, though very weak, felt disposed to continue his journey. We traveled fourteen miles to Germantown. He was quite sick at night, and the bilious fever seemed to be settled upon him. I was also very feeble myself.

On the day following, September 1st, being Sunday, Brother Taylor concluded to remain there for the day and hold a meeting.

It was a German settlement. He wished me to speak, and I spoke upon the first principles of the gospel. He followed me, and spoke until he was exhausted.

After we returned to the inn where we were stopping, I was taken with a chill and fever, and had a very bad night Brother Taylor was also very sick.

The following day, September 2nd, was a painful day to my feelings. It was evident that Brother Taylor had a settled fever upon him, and would not be able to travel. Father Coltrin was resolved to continue his journey, and, in conversing with Brother Taylor, he thought it better for one sick man to be left than for two, as I was so sick with the chills and fever that I was not able to render him any assistance, nor, indeed, to take care of myself. Under these circumstances, Brother Taylor advised me to continue my journey with Brother Coltrin, and make the best of my way to New York.

CHAPTER XXII.

CONTINUE MY JOURNEY — LEAVE ELDER TAYLOR IN GERMANTOWN — ARRIVE IN CLEVELAND—TAKE STEAMER FROM THERE TO BUFFALO—DELAYED BY A STORM—GO TO FARMINGTON, MY FATHER'S HOME—DEATH OF MY GRANDMOTHER—MY UNCLE DIES—I PREACH HIS FUNERAL SERMON--ARRIVE IN NEW YORK — SAIL FOR LIVERPOOL — ENCOUNTER STORMS AND ROUGH WEATHER —ARRIVE IN LIVERPOOL.

AFTER committing Elder Taylor into the hands of the Lord, though painful to me, I gave him the parting hand and started. I left him in Germantown, Wayne County, Indiana, in the hands of a merciful God and a kind and benevolent family; who promised to do everything in their power to make him comfortable until his recovery.

This they did, though he passed through a severe course of the bilious fever, and was sick nigh unto death.   Through the mercy of God, however, he recovered from his sickness, and continued his journey. We next met in the city of New York. I continued my journey with Father Coltrin, and we reached Cleveland on the 18th of Sep-tember. We there took a steamer for Buffalo, but were three days and a night in a storm before we made the harbor. We landed at midnight, and in doing so, we ran into a schooner, and stove it in.

From Buffalo, I traveled to Albany in a canal boat and had a stroke of' the ague daily.

While on the journey, at Albany I took a stage in the night and rode to my father's home in Farmington on the 21st of September.

I was glad to meet with my father's family and the other members of the small branch of the Church which existed there upon this occasion, as I found them all strong in the faith of the gospel, and glad to meet with me.

I was still suffering with the ague daily.

On the 27th of September, my grandmother (on my mother's side) Anna Thompson, died at Avon. She was eighty-four years of age.

It was a singular coincidence that she, with her husband, Lot Thompson, also Mercy Thompson and Samuel Thompson, all of one family, died when they were eighty-four years of age. I was not able to attend my grandmother's funeral.

On the 4th of October, 1839, my uncle, Adna Hart, died, aged forty-three years. I had visited him in his sickness, and preached the gospel to him, and he was believing. I had also been associated with him from my youth up.

On his death-bed he sent me a request that I would preach his funeral sermon.

I was having the chills and fever daily at the time, attended with a very severe cough, so much so that my father thought that I would never leave his home alive. But when they brought me the request of my dying uncle, and the day came for his burial, I told my father to get his horse and buggy ready for I was going to attend the funeral.

He thought I was very reckless in regard to my own life as I had suffered with the chills and fever some fifteen days, and to attempt to speak in my weak state, and to begin at the same hour that my chill was to come on, seemed to him foolhardy.

My parents were quite alarmed, yet according to my request my father got up his team and I rode with him and my step-mother five miles through a cold, chilly wind and I com-menced speaking to a large congregation at the same hour that my chill had been in the habit of coming on.

I spoke over an hour with great freedom, and my chill left me from that hour and I had no more attacks for many days.

On the Monday following, October 17th, I felt sufficiently restored to health to continue my journey. I took leave of my father and sister and left for New York, where I arrived on the morning of the 8th of November.

I spent two months and seven days after my arrival in New York in traveling and prea-ching in that city, New Jersey and Long Island—a portion of the this with Parley and Orson Pratt. I had frequent attacks during this time of the chills and fever, but I preached almost daily.

On the 13th of December, I attended our conference in New York City with Parley P. Pratt, and on this day Elder John Taylor arrived in our midst, and it was a happy meeting.

He had passed through a severe siege of sickness after we parted, but through the mercy of God had been preserved and was able to continue his journey. He also informed us that others of the quorum of the Twelve had suffered a great deal of sickness and that it was with difficulty that they could travel.

After spending six days in New York, Elder John Taylor, in company with Elder Theodore Turley and myself, sailed out of New York Harbor for Liverpool on board the packet ship Oxford on the 19th of December, 1839.

We took steerage passage which cost fifteen dollars each. We had storms and rough weather, but most of the winds were favorable for a quick passage.

While on the ship, a Methodist minister got into a discussion with some Catholics who were in the company, and the arguments of the minister ran rather more into abuse than sound argument.

Elder Taylor told the Methodist minister that he did not think it was becoming in a daughter to find so much fault with the mother as they did, for as the Methodists came out of the Catholics, Elder Taylor thought the mother had as much right to enjoy her religion unmolested as the daughter had. That ended the argument.

Our company consisted of 709 souls, composed of Americans, English, Scotch, Irish, Welsh and Dutch.

We arrived in Liverpool dock on the 11th day of January, 1840, having made the voyage from New York in twenty-three days.

CHAPTER XXIII.

OUR VISIT TO PRESTON — OUR FIRST COUNCIL IN ENGLAND, IN 1840—WE TAKE DIFFERENT FIELDS OP LABOR—A WOMAN POSSESSED OF THE DEVIL—ATTEMPT TO CAST IT OUT AND FAIL — TURN OUT THE UNBELIEVERS, AND THEN SUCCEED — THE EVIL SPIRIT ENTERS HER CHILD — COMMENCE BAPTIZING — THE LORD MAKES KNOWN HIS WILL TO ME.

ON January 13th, 1840, after visiting Mr. George Cannon, the father of President George Q. Cannon, and his family, we took cars in the evening and arrived in the midst of the Preston branch of the Saints, built up in 1837, by Elder Heber C. Kimball, Orson Hyde and Willard Richards.

We very soon had a pleasant interview with Elder Willard Richards who had remained in Preston to take care of the Church while the rest had returned home to America.

We spent three days at Preston in visiting the Saints, and on the 17th we held a council at Elder Richards' home in that place.

After consulting upon the best course for us to pursue, it was finally resolved that Elder Taylor and Joseph Fielding go to Liverpool, Elder Woodruff to Staffordshire Potteries, Theodore Turley to Birmingham, Elder Richards wherever the Spirit might direct him, and that Wm. Clayton preside over the branch in Manchester.

After various principles of the Church had been expounded by the Apostles present, the council adjourned.

Elder Willard Richards had been called to be one of the quorum of the Twelve Apostles, but had not yet received his ordination.

On the day following, I parted with Elders Taylor and Fielding who went to Liverpool, and with Elder Richards who tarried in Preston. Elder Turley and I went to Manchester.

It was the first time I ever visited that city. I here first met with Elder Wm. Clayton. As soon as I had an introduction to him, he informed me that one of the sisters in that place was possessed of the devil, and he asked me to go and cast it out of her, thinking that one of the Twelve Apostles could do anything in this line he might wish to.

However, I went with him to the house where the woman lay, in the hands of three men, in a terrible rage, and trying to tear her clothing from her.

I also found quite a number of Saints present, and some unbelievers who had come to see the devil cast out and a miracle wrought.

If I had acted upon my own judgment, I should not have attempted to administer to her with the company present but as I was a stranger there, and Brother Clayton presided over the branch, I joined him in administering to the woman. But the unbelief of the wicked present was so great that we could not cast the devil out of her, but she raged worse than ever.

I then ordered the room to be cleared and when the company left the house, except the few attending to her, we laid hands upon her and I commanded the devil to come out of her in the name of Jesus Christ. The devil left her and she was entirely cured and fell asleep.

The next day being the Sabbath, she came before a large congregation of people and bore testimony to what the Lord had done for her. We had a large assemblage through the day and evening to whom I preached the gospel.

On Monday morning, the devil not being satisfied with being cast out of the woman, entered into her little child which was but a few months old.

I was called upon to visit the child. I found it in great distress, writhing in its mother's arms. We laid hands upon it and cast the devil out of it and the evil spirits had no power over the household afterwards.

This was done by the power of God and not of man. We laid hands upon twenty in Manchester who were sick, and they were mostly healed.

On the 21st, I arrived in Burslem by coach and met for the first time, with Elder Alfred Cordon. This being my field of labor, I stopped and commenced work.

Elder Turley stopped in the pottery district some eight days, then went to Birmingham, his field of labor.

I received a letter on the 10th of February from Elder John Taylor, who was at Liverpool, saying they had commenced there and baptized ten persons.

I labored in the Staffordshire Potteries, in Burslem, Hanley, Stoke, Lane End, and several other villages, from the 2nd of January until the 2nd of March, preaching every night in the week and two or three times on the Sabbath.

I baptized, confirmed and blessed many, and we had a good field open for labor. Many were believing, and it appeared as though we had a door open to bring many into the Church in that part of the vineyard.

March 1st, 1840, was my birthday, when I was thirty-three years of age. It being Sunday, I preached twice through the day to a large assembly in the City Hall in the town of Hanley, and administered the sacrament unto the Saints.

In the evening, I again met with a large assembly of the Saints and strangers, and while singing the first hymn, the Spirit of the Lord rested upon me, and the voice of God said to me, "This is the last meeting that you will hold with this people for many days."

I was astonished at this, as I had many appointments out in that district.

When I arose to speak to the people, I told them that it was the last meeting I should hold with them for many days. They were as much astonished as I was.

At the close of the meeting, four persons came forward for baptism, and we went down into the water and baptized them.

In the morning, I went in secret before the Lord, and asked Him what His will was concerning me.

The answer I got was that I should go to the south, for the Lord had a great work for me to perform there, as many souls were waiting for the word of the Lord.

CHAPTER XXIV.

MY JOURNEY TO HEREFORDSHIRE—INTER-
VIEW WITH JOHN BENBOW—THE WORD OF
THE LORD FULFILLED TO ME — THE
GREATEST GATHERING INTO THE CHURCH
KNOWN AMONG THE GENTILES SINCE THE
ORGANIZATION OF THE CHURCH IN THIS
DISPENSATION — A CONSTABLE SENT TO
ARREST ME—I CONVERT AND BAPTIZE HIM—
TWO CLERKS SENT AS DETECTIVES TO HEAR
ME PREACH, AND BOTH EMBRACE THE
TRUTH — RECTORS PETITION TO HAVE
PREACHING PROHIBITED — THE ARCH-
BISHOP'S REPLY — PRINT BOOK OF MORMON
AND HYMN BOOK—CASE OF HEALING.

ON the 3rd of March, 1840, in fulfillment of
the word of the Lord to me, I took coach and rode
to Wolverhampton, twenty-six miles, and spent the
night there.

On the morning of the 4th, I again took a
coach and rode through Dudley, Stourbridge,
Stourport and Worcester, and then walked a
number of miles to Mr. John Benbow's Hill Farm,
Castle Frome, Ledbury, Herefordshire. This was a
farming country in the south of England, a region

where no Elder of the Latter-day Saints had visited.

I found Mr. Benbow to be a wealthy farmer, cultivating three hundred acres of land, occupying a good mansion, and having plenty of means. His wife, Jane, had no children.

I presented myself to him as a missionary from America, an Elder of the Church of Jesus Christ of Latter-day Saints, who had been sent to him by the commandment of God as a messenger of salvation, to preach the gospel of life unto him and his household and the inhabitants of the land.

Mr. Benbow and his wife received me with glad hearts and thanksgiving. It was in the evening when I arrived, having traveled forty-eight miles by coach and on foot during the day, but after receiving refreshments we sat down together, and conversed until two o'clock in the morning.

Mr. Benbow and his wife rejoiced greatly at the glad tidings which I brought unto them of the fullness of the everlasting gospel which God had revealed through the mouth of His Prophet, Joseph Smith in these last days.

I rejoiced greatly at the news that Mr. Benbow gave me that there was a company of men and women—over six hundred in number—who had broken off from the Wesleyan Methodists, and taken the name of United Brethren. They had forty-five preachers among them, and had chapels and many houses that were licensed according to the law of the land for preaching in.

This body of United Brethren were searching for light and truth, but had gone as far as they could, and were continually calling upon the Lord to open the way before them and send them light and knowledge that they might know the true way to be saved.

When I heard these things, I could clearly see why the Lord had commanded me, while in the town of Hanley, to leave that place of labor and go to the south, for in Herefordshire there was a great harvest-field for gathering many Saints into the kingdom of God.

I retired to my bed with joy after offering my prayers and thanksgiving to God, and slept sweetly until the rising of the sun.

I arose on the morning of the 5th, took breakfast, and told Mr. Benbow I would like to commence my Master's business by preaching the gospel to the people.

He had a large hall in his mansion which was licensed for preaching, and he sent word through the neighborhood that an American missionary would preach at his house that evening.

As the time drew nigh, many of the neighbors came in and I preached my first gospel sermon in the house. I also preached on the following evening at the same place and baptized six persons, including Mr. John Benbow and his wife, and four preachers of the United Brethren.

I spent most of the following day in cleaning out a pool of water and preparing it for baptizing in, as I saw many to be baptized there. I afterwards baptized six hundred in that pool of water.

On Sunday the 8th, I preached at Frome's Hill in the morning, at Standley Hill in the afternoon, and at John Benbow's Hill Farm in the evening.

The parish church that stood in the neighborhood of Brother Benbow's, presided over by the rector of the parish, was attended during the day by only fifteen persons, while I had a large congregation, estimated to number a thousand, attend my meeting through the day and evening.

When I arose in the evening to speak at Brother Benbow's house, a man entered the door and informed me that he was a constable, and had been sent by the rector of the parish with a warrant to arrest me.

I asked him, "For what crime?"

He said, "For preaching to the people."

I told him that I, as well as the rector, had a license for preaching the gospel to the people, and that if he would take a chair I would wait upon him after meeting.

He took my chair and sat beside me. I preached the first principles of the everlasting gospel for an hour and a quarter. The power of God rested upon me, the Spirit filled the house, and the people were convinced.

At the close of the meeting, I opened a door for baptism, and seven offered themselves. Among the number were four preachers and the constable.

The latter arose and said, "Mr. Woodruff, I would like to be baptized."

I told him I would like to baptize him. I went down to the pool and baptized the seven. We then met together and I confirmed thirteen, and broke bread unto the Saints and we all rejoiced together.

The constable went to the rector and told him if he wanted Mr. Woodruff taken up for preaching the gospel, he must go himself and serve the writ, for he had heard him preach the only true gospel sermon he had ever listened to in his life.

The rector did not know what to make of it, so he sent two clerks of the Church of England as spies, to attend our meeting, and find out what we did preach.

But they were both pricked in their hearts and received the word of the Lord gladly, and were baptized and confirmed members of the Church of Jesus Christ of Latter-day Saints.

The rector became alarmed and did not dare to send anybody else.

The ministers and rectors of the South of England called a convention and sent a petition to the Archbishop of Canterbury, to request parliament to pass a law prohibiting the "Mormons" from preaching in the British dominion.

In this petition the rector stated that one "Mormon" missionary had baptized fifteen hundred persons, mostly members of the English church, during the last seven months.

But the archbishop and council, knowing well that the laws of England gave free toleration to all religions under the British flag, sent word to the petitioners that if they had the worth of souls at heart as much as they had the ground where hares, foxes and hounds ran, they would not lose so many of their flock.

I continued to preach and baptize daily.

On the 21st day of March, I baptized Elder Thomas Kingston. He was the superintendent of both preachers and members of the United Brethren.

The first thirty days after my arrival in Herefordshire, I had baptized forty-five preachers and one hundred-and-sixty members of the United Brethren, who put into my hands one chapel and forty-five houses, which were licensed according to law to preach in.

This opened a wide field for labor, and enabled me to bring into the Church, through the blessing of God, over eighteen hundred souls during eight months, including all of the six hundred United Brethren except one person; also including some two hundred preachers of the various denominations.

This field of labor embraced Hereford-shire, Gloucestershire and Worcestershire, and formed the conferences of Garway, Godfield Elm and Frome's Hill.

I was visited by President Young and Dr. Richards.

Brother Benbow furnished us with £300 to print the first Book of Mormon that was published in England; and on the 20th of May, l840, Brigham Young, Willard Richards and I held a council on the top of Malvern Hill, and there decided that Brigham Young go direct to Manchester and publish 3,000 copies of the Hymn Book and 3,000 copies of the Book of Mormon, this being the first publication of these books in England.

The power of God rested upon us and upon the mission.

The sick were healed, devils were cast out, and the lame were made to walk.

One case I will mention: Mary Pitt, who died in Nauvoo, sister to Wm. Pitt, who died in Salt Lake City, had not walked upon her feet for eleven years. We carried her into the water, and I baptized her.

On the evening of the 18th of May, l840, at Brother Kingston's house in Dymock, Elders Brigham Young, Willard Ricbards and I laid hands upon her head and confirmed her.

Brigham Young, being mouth, rebuked her lameness and commanded her to arise and walk in the name of the Lord. The lameness then left her, and she never afterwards used a staff or crutch.

She walked through the town of Dymock next day, which created a stir among the people; but the wicked did not feel to give God the glory.

The whole history of this Herefordshire mission shows the importance of listening to the still small voice of the Spirit of God and the revelations of the Holy Ghost.

The Lord had a people there prepared for the gospel. They were praying for light and truth, and the Lord sent me to them, and I declared the gospel of life and salvation unto them, and some eighteen hundred souls received it, and many of them have been gathered to Zion in these mountains. Many of them have also been called to officiate in the bishopric and have done much good in Zion. But in all these things we should ever acknowledge the hand of God, and give him the honor, praise and glory, forever and ever. Amen.

CHAPTER XXV.

CLOSING TESTIMONY — GOOD AND EVIL SPIRITS.

BEFORE closing this little book as a reader for our children, I wish to bear my testimony upon several principles to the Latter-day Saints, especially to the rising generation, the young men of Israel.

First, I wish to speak of the spirits of good and evil. The Lord says, whatever leads to good is of God, and whatever leads to do evil is of the devil. This is a very important subject for us to understand.

The scriptures again tell us that there arc many spirits gone out into the world; and that we should try the spirits, to prove which are of God and which are of the evil one. The New Testament says that every spirit that confesses that Jesus is the Christ, is born of God; and every spirit that denieth that Jesus is the Christ is anti-Christ, and is not of God. I will also add that every spirit that confesses that Joseph Smith was a prophet of God, and that the Book of Mormon, Bible and Doctrine and Covenants are true is of God; and every spirit that denieth this is not of God but is of the evil one.

I wish here to ask our young friends as well as the older ones, the question: Do you ever consider or contemplate anything about the number of evil spirits that occupy the earth, who are at war against God and against all good, and who seek to destroy all the children of men in every age of the world?

Let us reason together a moment upon this subject. It may be impossible for any man without direct revelation from God, to get to know the exact number, but we may approximate towards it.

The Lord has said by revelation that Lucifer, an angel in authority, rebelled against God and drew away one-third part of the hosts of heaven; and he was cast down to the earth, and the heavens wept over him.

How many were cast out of heaven down to the earth? We suppose that the inhabitants of heaven here referred to were the spirits begotten of our Father in heaven who were to come down to the earth and take tabernacles. How many were there to come down and take tabernacles? This, again, may be difficult to tell, yet perhaps we may come near enough for the purpose. It has generally been conceded that there are about 1,000,000,000 persons on the earth at a time, though the late statistics make out 1,400,000,000 at the present time. But we will say 1,000,000,000. It is also said that a generation passes off the earth every thirty-three and one-third years, making three generations in a century, which would be 3,000,000,000 in one hundred years. Multiply this by ten and it will make 30,000,000,000 in l,000 years. Multiply again by seven and it will make 210,000,000,000 in 7,000 years.

The argument might be used that when our earth was first peopled, there were but two persons on the earth, and after the flood but eight souls were left alive; but the probability is that during the millennium, the inhabitants will increase very fast as the age of children will be as the age of a tree, and the inhabitants of the earth will not die off as they do now.

But we will suppose that there were 100,000,000,000 of fallen spirits sent down from heaven to earth, and that there are 1,000,000,000 of inhabitants upon the face of the earth to-day, that would make one hundred evil spirits to every man, woman and child living on the earth; and the whole mission and labor of these spirits is to lead all the children of men to do evil and to effect their destruction.

Now, I want all our boys and girls to reflect upon this, and to see what danger they are in, and the warfare they have to pass through.

These one hundred evil spirits to each one of the children of men seek to lead them into every temptation possible, to use tobacco, smoke, drink whisky, get drunk, curse, swear, lie steal and commit adultery and murder, and do every evil to cut them off from exaltation as far as possible.

On the other hand, the Spirit of God labors and strives to preserve all the children of men from these evils; and the Lord has given His angels charge concerning us, and they do all they can for our salvation.

But yet we all have our agency to choose the good and refuse the evil, or to choose the evil and refuse the good. The Lord forces no man to heaven; neither does the Lord tempt any man to do evil. When a man is tempted to do evil, it is by the power of the devil, who is an enemy to all righteousness.

I feel very anxious to have our boy s and girls, our young men and maidens, seek for that which is good.

Whenever you are tempted to do evil, turn from it. Never make light of any of the commandments or ordinances of the gospel of Christ, and when you meet with any persons who do it, shun their society.

Avoid the use of tobacco and strong drink for they lead to evil.

You are laying the foundation while in the days of your youth, for a character which will decide your destiny through all time and throughout all eternity, either for good or evil.

The Lord has told us by revelation (See *Doc. and Cov.* sec. 130) that whatever knowledge on principle or intelligence we attain to in this life, it w ill rise with us in the resurrection, and any person who gains more knowledge and intelligence in this life through his diligence and obedience than another, will have so much the advantage in the world to come.

Therefore, we should all strive to be diligent in obtaining intelligence, and bringing to pass righteousness upon our agency, and not wait to be commanded in all things, and great will be our reward for so doing.

CHAPTER XXVI.

HOW TO OBTAIN REVELATIONS FROM GOD— JOSEPH SMITH'S COURSE — SAVED FROM DEATH BY A FALLING TREE, BY OBEYING THE VOICE OF THE SPIRIT — A COMPANY OF SAINTS SAVED FROM A STEAMBOAT DISASTER BY THE SPIRIT'S WARNING—PLOT TO WAYLAY ELDER C. C. RICH AND PARTY FOILED BY THE SAME POWER.

IN order to obtain revelation from God and in order to know when we do obtain a revelation, whether it is from God or not, we must follow the teachings of the revelations of God unto us. St. James says: "If any man lack wisdom, let him ask of God, that giveth to all men liberally, and upbraideth not; and it shall be given him." Again, it is said, "Ask, and it shall be given you; seek, and ye shall find; knock and it shall be opened unto you."

It was upon this promise that Joseph Smith went before the Lord and prayed in the name of Jesus Christ and asked for knowledge, wisdom and understanding, in order to know what to do to be saved; and he proved the promise of St. James before the Lord, and the heavens were opened to his view and the Father and Son were revealed unto him and the voice of the great Eloheim unto him was: "This is my beloved Son, hear ye Him."

This was the first revelation of God to him. He did hearken to the voice of Jesus Christ all his life afterwards and received a code of revelations and the word of the Lord unto him as long as he dwelt in the flesh.

Joseph Smith left as strong a testimony as was ever given to the human family, and sealed that testament with his own life and blood.

We all have to pursue the same course in order to obtain revelations from God. But I wish to impress this truth upon the rising generation and all who read this testimony, that the Lord does not give revelations or send angels to men or work miracles to accommo-date the notions of any man who is seeking for a sign.

When we have the principles of the gospel revealed to us through the mouth of the Savior, or by inspired prophets or apostles, we have no need to ask the Lord to reveal that unto us again. While the priesthood is restored to the earth, and the revelations of God are revealed to us through the mouths of prophets and apostles concerning the fullness of the gospel—doctrine, ordinances and principles, we should study them and treasure up knowledge by faith. We should study out of the best books, and the Holy Ghost will bring to our remembrance those things which we stand in need of, in the self same hour that we are called to teach the people.

But when any priest, elder, prophet, apostle or messenger is sent of God to preach the gospel, gather the Saints, work in temples, or perform any work for the Lord, and that man is faithful and humble before the Lord, in his prayers and duty, and there is any snare or evil in his path, or the righteous to be sought out, or danger to the emigration of the Saints either by sea or by land, or knowledge needed in a temple, then the Lord will reveal to him all that is necessary to meet the emergency.

The teachings of the prophet Joseph Smith to President John Taylor and the rest of us, was to obtain the Holy Spirit, get acquainted with it and its operations, and listen to the whisperings of that Spirit and obey its voice, and it soon would become a principle of revelation unto us.

We have found this true in our experience, and in order to prove whether a revelation is from God or not we follow out the principles revealed to us, and if we find that which was manifested to us proved true, we know it was from God; for truth is one of His attributes, and the Holy Ghost deceiveth no man. When a man becomes acquainted with the whisperings of the Holy Ghost, which is revelation, he should be very careful to obey it, for his life may depend upon it.

Revelation is one of the gifts of the Holy Ghost, and for the benefit of my young friends who may read this work, I will give an account of a few instances from my own experience of listening to the revelations of the Holy Ghost to me.

In 1848, after my return to Winter Quarters from our pioneer journey, I was appointed by the Presidency of the Church to take my family and go to Boston to gather up the remnant of the Latter-day Saints and lead them to the valleys of the mountains.

While on my way east, I put my carriage into the yard of one of the brethren in Indiana, and Brother Orson Hyde set his wagon by the side of mine, and not more than two feet from it.

Dominicus Carter, of Provo, and my wife and four children were with me. My wife, one child and I went to bed in the carriage, the rest sleeping in the house.

I had been in bed but a short time when a voice said to me: "Get up, and move your carriage."

It was not thunder, lightning or an earthquake, but the still, small voice of the Spirit of God—the Holy Ghost.

I told my wife I must get up and move my carriage. She asked: "What for?"

I told her I did not know, only the Spirit told me to do it.

I got up and moved my carriage several rods, and set it by the side of the house.

As I was returning to bed the same Spirit said to me, "Go and move your mules away from that oak tree," which was about one hundred yards north of our carriage.

I moved them to a young hickory grove and tied them up. I then went to bed.

In thirty minutes, a whirlwind caught the tree to which my mules had been fastened, broke it off near the ground, and carried it one hundred yards, sweeping away two fences in its course, and laid it prostrate through that yard where my carriage stood, and the top limbs hit my carriage as it was.

In the morning, I measured the trunk of the tree which fell where my carriage had stood, and I found it to be five feet in diameter. It came within a foot of Brother Hyde's wagon but did not touch it.

Thus, by obeying the revelation of the Spirit of God to me, I saved my life and the lives of my wife and child, as well as my animals.

In the morning, I went on my way rejoicing.

While returning to Utah in 1850 with a large company of Saints from Boston and the east, on my arrival at Pittsburgh I engaged a passage for myself and company on a steamer to St. Louis. But no sooner had I engaged the passage than the Spirit said to me, "Go not on board of that steamer, neither you nor your company."

I obeyed the revelation to me and did not go on board, but took another steamer.

The first steamer started at dark, with 200 passengers on board. When five miles down the Ohio River, it took fire, burned the tiller ropes so that the vessel could not reach shore, and the lives of nearly all on board were lost either by fire or water. We arrived in safety at our destination, by obeying the revelation of the Spirit of God to us.

In another instance, after attending a large annual conference in Salt Lake City and, having had a good deal of business to attend to, I was somewhat weary; and at the close of the conference, I thought I would repair to my home and have a rest.

As I went into the yard the Spirit said to me, "Take your team and go to the farm," which is some three miles south of the tabernacle.

As I was hitching the horses to the wagon, Mrs. Woodruff asked where I was going.

I said, "To the farm."

"What for?" she asked.

"I do not know," I replied; but when I arrived there I found out. The creek had overf-lowed, broken through my ditch, surrounded my home and filled my barn-yard and pig pen. My wife was wading in the water trying to turn it from the lot to save the home and family.

Through my own exertions I soon turned it, and prevented much damage that might have occurred had I not obeyed the voice of the Spirit.

This same spirit of revelation has been manifested to many of my brethren in their labors in the kingdom of God, one of which I will here name.

Elder Chas. C. Rich was going from Sacramento to San Bernardino with a company of the brethren. He had in his possession a large amount of money to make payment on their land purchase. This was known to some road agents in the vicinity, who gathered a company of robbers and went on ahead of Brother Rich and lay in ambush, intending to kill the Mormons and rob them of their money.

Before reaching the company of robbers, Brother Rich came to a by-path or trail. The Spirit then told him to take that path.

The brethren with him marveled at his course, not knowing that enemies awaited them, but they arrived in safety at San Bernardino with their lives and money, while the robbers wondered why their prey did not come.

CHAPTER XXVII.

RESULT OF NOT OBEYING THE VOICE OF THE SPIRIT—LOST IN A SNOWSTORM—SAVED IN ANSWER TO PRAYER — REVELATION TO MISSIONARIES NECESSARY — REVELATIONS IN THE ST. GEORGE TEMPLE.

I WILL now give an example from my own experience of the result of not obeying the voice of the Spirit.

Some years since I had a part of my family living in Randolph, Rich County. I was there on a visit with my team, in the month of December.

One Monday morning, my monitor, the Spirit watching over me, said, "Take your team and go home to Salt Lake City."

When I named it to my family who were at Randolph, they urged me very strongly to stop longer.

Through their persuasion, I stayed until Saturday morning with the Spirit continually prompting me to go home. I then began to feel ashamed to think that I had not obeyed the whisperings of the Sprit to me before.

I took my team and started early on Saturday morning. When I arrived at Woodruff, the Bishop urged me to stop until Monday and he would go with me.

I told him, "No, I have tarried too long already."

I drove on sprightly, and when within fifteen miles of Wasatch, a furious snow storm over-took me, the wind blowing heavily in my face.

For fifteen minutes, I could not see any road whatever, and knew not how or where to guide my horses.

I left my lines loosely on my animals, went inside my wagon, tied down the cover, and committed my life and guidance into the hands of the Lord, trusting to my horses to find the way as they had twice before passed over that road.

I prayed to the Lord to forgive my sin in not obeying the voice of the Spirit to me and implored

Him to preserve my life.

My horses brought me into the Wasatch station at 9 o'clock in the evening, with the hubs of my wagon dragging in the snow.

I got my horses under cover, and had to remain there until the next Monday night, with the snow six feet deep on the level and still snowing.

It was with great difficulty at last that I saved the lives of my horses by getting them into a box car and taking them to Ogden; while if I had obeyed the revelation of the Spirit of God to me, I should have traveled to Salt Lake City over a good road without any storm.

As I have received the good and the evil, the fruits of obedience and disobedience, I think I am justified in exhorting all my young friends to always obey the whisperings of the Spirit of God, and then they will always be safe.

The Spirit of God will rule over and guide all men who will permit it and seek for it, and this is especially necessary for young Elders who are laboring in the vineyard of the Lord. For the Lord knows where the righteous, honest and meek of the earth are and will lead the Elders to them.

I have already related a remarkable instance of this in my own experience when the voice of the Lord came to me in the town of Hanley, England, in 1840.

In that case, it dictated me quite contrary to my expectations, for I had appointments out for a week ahead. But I obeyed the voice of the Spirit, went south as I was directed to, and my readers know the result.

I will refer to one more instance in my experience upon the subject of revelation:

All the Latter-day Saints understand that we build temples for the purpose of admini-stering ordinances for the dead as well as for the living.

The Lord has opened the way in a remarkable manner for many of the members of the Church to obtain records of the names of their dead for several generations.

I had also obtained a record of somewhat over 3,000 of my father's and mother's families.

After the dedication of the temple at St. George, President Young appointed me to preside over it. When we commenced work in the temple, I began to reflect: "How can I redeem my dead, I have some 3,000 names of the dead who have been baptized for, and how can I get endowments for them.

I had none of my family there, and if they had been there they would not have been able to get endowments for so many.

While praying to the Lord to show me how to redeem my dead, the Spirit of God rested upon me, and the voice of the Spirit said to me, "Go and call upon the sons and the daughters of Zion in St.

George, to come into the temple of the Lord and get their endowments for your dead; and it shall be acceptable unto me, saith the Lord."

This filled my soul with joy, and I saw that it opened a field as wide as eternity for the salvation of our dead and the redemption of man, that we might magnify our calling as saviors upon Mount Zion.

On my birthday, March I, 1877, the day that I was 70 years old, 154 sisters at St. George went into the temple to get endowments for the same number of the female portion of my dead.

This principle was received by President Young and adopted from that hour, and through the kindness of friends, I have had nearly 2,000 of my friends receive endowments in the temple of the Lord; and thousands of others have received the same blessings in the same way.

President Young received revelations in that temple, and there are yet many revelations to be received in the last days concerning the redemption of the dead and many other subjects, but they will all be manifest in due time through the proper authority unto the Church and kingdom of God.

There are many other manifestations of the power of God and the revelations of Jesus Christ to us in our lives. We have been called by revelation to give endowments for many persons now dead, who, when living, were honorable men of the earth, and some who were prominent in our nation, but who were not members of our family.

But I have said sufficient upon this branch of the subject.

CHAPTER XXVIII.

PATRIARCHAL BLESSINGS AND THEIR FULFILLMENT—PREDICTIONS IN MY OWN BLESSING—GOLD DUST FROM CALIFORNIA — TAUGHT BY AN ANGEL—STRUGGLE WITH EVIL SPIRITS—ADMINISTERED TO BY ANGELS —WHAT ANGELS ARE SENT TO THE EARTH FOR.

THE duty of a Patriarch is to bestow blessings upon his posterity and the children of men.

In a revelation (*Doc. and Cov.* sec. 107), the Lord says that "Three years previous to the death of Adam, he called Seth, Enos, Cainan, Mahalaleel, Jared, Enoch and Methuselah who were all High Priests, with the residue of his posterity who were righteous, into the valley of Adam-ondi-Ahman, and there bestowed upon them his last blessing. * * * * And Adam * * * predicted whatsoever should befall his posterity unto the last gene-ration. These things are all written in the book of Enoch, and are to be testified of in due time."

Abraham, Isaac and Jacob were Patriarchs, and blessed their posterity. All that Jacob said and sealed upon the heads of his twelve sons has been fulfilled to the very letter, as far as time has permitted.

We also have Patriarchs in our day. Father Joseph Smith, the father of the Prophet Joseph Smith, was the first Patriarch in the Church of Jesus Christ of Latter-day Saints. He gave a great many blessings unto the Saints, which are recorded, and many of them have seen their fulfillment.

When he put his hands on the head of a person to bless him, it seemed as though the heavens were opened, and he could reveal the whole life of that person.

He gave me my patriarchal blessing in the temple of the Lord at Kirtland, on the 15th day of April, 1837. Many marvelous things which he sealed upon my head, for which I could then see no earthly chance of fulfillment, have already been fulfilled to the very letter.

One or two instances I will name. He said I should have access to treasures hid in the ground to assist me in getting myself and others to Zion.

When in Cambridgeport gathering up the Saints in 1850, Alexander Badlam went to California on business, and the Saints who were digging gold filled a little sack with gold dust and sent it to me to assist me on my mission. By the sale of this treasure from California, I was enabled to emigrate myself, family and a number of others to Zion in the mountains.

He also said I should have power to bring my father and his family into the Church. This was fulfilled when I visited them during my mission to the Fox Islands, as previously related.

My father gathered to Salt Lake City with the Saints and he died there, aged 83 years.

The Patriarch also said I should be wrapt in the visions of heaven, and an angel of God should teach me many things. This was literally fulfilled.

Again, he told me I should be delivered from my enemies (who would seek my destruction) by the mighty power of God and the administrations of angels. This was marvelously fulfilled while in the city of London in 1840. Brothers Heber C. Kimball, Geo. A. Smith and I went to London together in the winter of 1840, being the first Elders who had attempted to establish the gospel in that great and mighty city. As soon as we commenced, we found the devil was manifest; the evil spirits gathered for our destruction and at times they had great power.

They would destroy all the Saints if they were not restrained by the power of God.

Brother Smith and myself were together and had retired to our rest, each occupying a cot but three feet apart. We had only just lain down, when it seemed as if a legion of devils made war upon us, to destroy us, and we were struggling for our lives in the midst of this warfare of evil spirits until we were nearly choked to death. I began to pray the best that I could in the midst of this struggle and asked the Father in the name of Jesus Christ to spare our lives.

While thus praying, three personages entered the room clothed in white and encircled with light.

They walked to our bedside, laid hands upon our heads and we were instantly delivered; and from that time forth we were no more trou-bled with evil spirits while in the city of London.

As soon as they administered unto us, they withdrew from the room, the lights withdrew with them and darkness returned.

Many other sayings of the Patriarch Joseph Smith in my blessing have been fulfilled in my experience, but I have said sufficient upon this subject. All the blessings that are sealed upon our heads will be fulfilled, and many more, if we are faithful and live for them.

In closing my testimony, I wish to say that I do not think that the Lord ever sends an angel to the earth to visit the children of men unless it is necessary to introduce a dispensation of the gospel, or deliver a message, or perform a work that cannot be done otherwise.

It required an angel of God to deliver the gospel to Joseph Smith because it was not then upon the earth, and that was in fulfillment of the word of the Lord through John the Revelator (*Revelations xiv*. 6). And so in regard to the administration of angels in all ages of the world; it is to deliver a message and perform a work which cannot otherwise be accomplished.

More reading from Archive Publishers:

The Great Apostasy (James E. Talmadge)	10.95
The Mediation & Atonement of Jesus Christ (John Taylor)	11.95
The Government of God (John Taylor)	7.95
Martyrdom of Joseph Smith & The Mormons (Taylor/Kane)	6.95
A Concise History of the Mormon Battalion (Daniel Tyler)	18.95
The Book of John Whitmer (John Whitmer)	7.95
The Mormon Prophet's Tragedy (Orson F. Whitney)	7.95
Joseph Smith as Scientist (John A. Widtsoe)	10.95
White Indian Boy/Uncle "Nick" (Elijah N. Wilson)	12.95
The Life of David Patten (Lycurgus A. Wilson)	6.95
The Memoirs of John R. Young (John R. Young)	18.95
A Collection of Deseret's Pioneer Histories	6.95
Lectures on Faith (1835 Edition)	5.95
The New Testament Apocrypha	13.95
The Book of Jasher	13.95
The Book of Enoch	11.95

Books from the FAITH-PROMOTING SERIES

The Life of Nephi (George Q. Cannon)	9.95
My First Mission (George Q. Cannon)	6.95
A String of Pearls (George Q. Cannon, ed.)	8.95
Heber C. Kimball's Journal (Heber C. Kimball)	7.95
Early Scenes from Church History (George C. Lambert)	6.95
Suffering and Service of Thomas Briggs (George C. Lambert)	6.95
Jacob Hamblin (James A. Little)	10.95
The Spaulding Manuscript (Reynolds/Spaulding)	12.95
Leaves from My Journal (Wilford Woodruff)	10.95
Leaves from My Journal Workbook (Woodruff/Monnett)	13.95
Fragments of Experience	8.95
Scraps pf Biography	8.95

www.archivepublishers.com
www.spectre.com/ldsarchive
email: info@archivepublishers.com
Telephone: (435) 884-1072
Fax: (435) 884-1303

Archive Publishers
P. O. Box 1476
Grantsville, UT 84029